JANE DOONAN

Looking at Pictures in Picture Books

 Thimble Press

Looking at Pictures in Picture Books
comes from The Thimble Press
publishers since 1970 of *Signal*, the thrice-yearly
specialist journal devoted to books and reading for
children and young people

First published 1993
357910864

Copyright © Jane Doonan 1993

ISBN 0 903355 40 X

Keyed at The Thimble Press
Lockwood, Station Road, South Woodchester
Stroud, Glos. GL5 5EQ
Typesetting by Avonset, Midsomer Norton, Bath
Printed in Great Britain by
Short Run Press, Exeter

Jane ... on ... is ... of ... .ish an. l drama at a comprehensive school in Bath and is an associate tutor in the School of Education, University of Bath. She writes: 'I've been looking at pictures for as long as I can remember. My father made me my first bed and painted a narrative picture on the footboard: a bed to delight the eye and tell stories. He was a Sunday painter and took me to exhibitions instead of my mother, who was too busy reading. As a student of art history and English at university, I was drawn to works that did not fit neatly into a form: complex, intriguing fusions. My research centred on medieval alabaster altar-pieces – mass produced and exported in great numbers – which have a narrative function, are painted and three-dimensional, but are neither paintings nor sculpture. Ten years ago a children's literature course re-introduced me to picture books, which I had taken for granted when my children were young but which have proved to be the most intriguing fusions of all.'

Jane Doonan has written several studies of picture books for *Signal*, among them Anthony Browne's *Hansel and Gretel*, Maurice Sendak's *Outside Over There* and Robert Ingpen's *The Idle Bear*. (A complete listing of her *Signal* articles and their availability may be obtained from the Thimble Press.) She contributed 'The Object Lesson: Picture Books of Anthony Browne' to the journal *Word and Image* in 1986 and 'Aesthetic Dimensions: Satoshi Kitamura' to the American annual *Children's Literature* (Yale University Press, 1991).

In one of the rooms, he found some
coloured pencils. "Good," said Woolly.
"I'll do some drawing."

*The 'hinge illustration' (Jane Doonan's phrase; see page 32)
in* **When Sheep Cannot Sleep** *© 1986 Satoshi Kitamura*

CONTENTS

ACKNOWLEDGEMENTS

I have drawn on *Painting: Some Basic Principles* by Frederick Gore, Studio Vista, 1965, for some of the technical terms and points on composition.

The terms and discussion on how symbols are able to refer, by denotation and exemplification, and what constitutes an aesthetic object and an aesthetic attitude are based on material in the works of Nelson Goodman (see 'On the Bookshelf', page 77).

I developed some of the material in the section on close looking at *When Sheep Cannot Sleep* for tutorial sessions in the Arts Council Children's Literature Summer School held at Westminster College, Oxford, 1991.

Cover illustration **Cloudy** © *1989 Deborah King*
(see 'Close Looking in Action', pages 40-41)

Introduction

This book celebrates the pleasures, challenges and rewards of looking at pictures as part of the total experience of reading a picture book. Every experienced reader is confident with written material, but how pictorial art communicates is, for many, unfamiliar territory. While this does not affect our delight in picture books, it certainly limits our understanding of them. What I will try to provide, therefore, is some practical help so that the artist's contribution becomes easier to recognize and appreciate.

There are several views about the value of a book's visual element to a child, and no doubt they overlap to a certain extent. The most obvious one is that pictures, especially through their colour, provide children with sensuous pleasure for the eye: an affective visual experience. Another common view is that pictures are a means to an end – an aid to literacy and language development, whether for naming the parts or telling the tales – and as such are valued for providing a verbal experience. A less common view, and the one I believe honours the picture book most fully, holds that pictures, through their expressive powers, enable the book to function as an art object: something which gives form to ideas and to which we can attach our ideas. The value in this case lies in the aesthetic experience and the contribution the picture book can make to our aesthetic development.

In an aesthetic experience we are engaged in play of the most enjoyable and demanding kind. By playing with the ideas provoked by a work of art, we create something of our own from it. And in that play we have had to deal with abstract concepts logically, intuitively and imaginatively.

I am not claiming that, in order for a child to enjoy reading a picture book, he must learn to see more in the pictures than what is necessary for an understanding of the story on the simplest literary level. Naturally a young child cuddled up on a parent's lap will enjoy being read to and looking at the pictures. And in the primary classroom illustrated books may well inspire a love of books and learning to read. But why stop there? Let's consider some of the possibilities offered by pictures.

Figurative pictures represent a real or imaginary world.

Pictures are expressive, being vehicles for the artist's expression as well as artifacts that stimulate personal expressive response in the beholder.

Pictures are histories of style and form.

Pictures reflect the values of the society that produces and 'uses' them.

Pictures offer opportunities for the act of creation (for their maker) and re-creation (for their beholder).

How much help do children need to realize the possibilities of pictures? Certainly they respond to the expressive dimension and can talk about their impressions, but to move to the stage of relating impressions to the possible reasons for them, knowledge is needed: immersion is not enough. There is an important stage in a person's aesthetic development that depends upon having insights about the ways in which pictures may be interpreted.

Most of the material in this book is concerned with the crucial step beyond taking what pictures denote or literally represent to having some grasp upon how pictures are able to express and metaphorically display what cannot be pictured directly – ideas, moods, abstract notions and qualities.

Interpreting pictures fully involves attending to everything which presents itself to the eye. It is not necessarily obvious that the qualities of a picture come from the artist's style, choice of materials and compositions, nor how these pictorial means achieve their effects. Once children have been told and shown how lines and shapes and colours are able to refer to ideas and feelings, they can explore the dimension beyond what is literally represented. They move into partnership with the artist through the picture itself.

Interpretation also extends to the way a particular artist's style, or a particular picture book, relates to tradition (probably with some adult prompting – 'Have you seen this kind of picture before?' 'Does this remind you of any other picture books?'). A further insight for a child to grasp is that an artist expresses the values of her or his society.

Whether we are skilled or unskilled in interpretation, we make judgements as we move away from a painting or close the covers of a picture book. But the more ideas we have to play with, the more ideas we have found to play with, the greater is our understanding and the clearer our judgement.

Responding to a picture book as an art object sounds ambitious, but it is not beyond the interests and abilities of many children in school. Almost without exception an older child begins by assuming that reading a picture book is a very soft option, largely because she hasn't ever reflected on how much there is to consider: the object itself in all aspects of its physical form, and how words tell, and how pictures show, and what happens among the three of them, and what happens between them and the reader.

As a reader, she is the manipulator of the physical object, which in turn manipulates her emotions, raises and satisfies her curiosity. She is the reader of the words travelling through the text, but because it is a *picture* book, she is not required to make her own image of the fictional world, so she is not entirely a reader in the literary sense of the term. She is the beholder* of the pictures, looking at what is depicted and being affected by the interwoven arrangements that meet her eyes. And there is the synthesis of the picture-book experience, with object, words and images uniting in the composite text – the work that exists only in her mind.

Once a child discovers how much there is to be made from looking into pictures, reading a picture book becomes wonderfully taxing.

*I use 'beholder' because there is no established term to describe someone with formal understanding of visual images that are not free-standing works of art or one-off decorations but sequences of scenes, comic-book frames, illustrations in books. To call such a person a reader, and the skill visual literacy, would be convenient but fails to acknowledge the difference between the ways we receive written words and pictorial images.

I have arranged my material so that it moves from individual practice to the use of picture books with children in the classroom. 'Close Looking in General' and 'Close Looking in Context' cover what it is useful to know in order to be able to take an aesthetic attitude to the pictures in picture books. Next comes 'Close Looking in Action' with Satoshi Kitamura's *When Sheep Cannot Sleep* and Deborah King's *Cloudy*. Then we go 'Into the Classroom' with notes on how I have shared picture books with pupils and extracts from their written responses. 'On the Bookshelf' refers to some of the books I have found useful in my attempts to understand pictures and picture books. The 'Summary of Useful Terms' provides the basis for a working vocabulary and is illustrated by reference to well-known picture-book artists and their work.

Close Looking in General

What does it mean to take an aesthetic attitude towards a picture and, by extension, a sequence of pictures in a picture book? It means *doing* something: being active rather than passive. Unfortunately for art, there is a widely held notion that visual contemplation somehow doesn't engage our brains, but being able to make 'deeper meaning' from a picture, rather than just settling for impressions or for what it represents, involves us emotionally and cognitively. Since they cannot tell us directly or exactly what their signs mean, pictures present something of a puzzle, and our attitude to them must, above all, be open-minded.

Let us take a specific example: Maurice Sendak's *Outside Over There*. We have to be willing to scrutinize each picture and the sequence of pictures over and over again, even when we don't really understand them. There is no guarantee that we will be able to 'make sense' of all we are being shown. We have to start by saying, 'Maybe it's about a little girl who fails to look after her baby sister properly,' and follow that idea through from the first to the last page opening. If we subsequently discover too many enigmatic details and incidents to support that simple hypothesis, we may have to abandon it and start looking all over again. Why are the goblins faceless? What are we to make of the father figure? Is it Father who sits on the strand beside the ship? Or his ghost? Is he dead? Certainly we have to tolerate ambiguity. We may decide we know just what to make of Ida's story, then read that Sendak says it's the baby's story anyway, and a homage to Mozart. Such a radically different interpretation might well send us back to the picture book with a fresh viewpoint and a synopsis and recording of *The Magic Flute*. We may settle for several interpretations and feel satisfied with them all. Or none. What is crucial throughout all the searching, testing and hypothesizing is that we remain genuinely open-minded and prepared to give the whole process plenty of time.

Given that an understanding of how visual art communicates is central to regarding a picture book as an aesthetic object, and that open-mindedness is the key to our attitude, what knowledge do we need for our feelings to work upon? The more the better, obviously, because that's bound to make a difference to the varieties of meaning we can make. Something of the following would be helpful:

> – an awareness that every mark displayed in a picture is a potential carrier of meaning, beginning with the chosen material or medium and how the mark is made
> – knowledge about the basic ingredients of pictorial art and composition
> – knowledge about how pictorial symbols are able to refer both to entities which we can encounter in the real world and to abstract ideas and experiences
> – a working vocabulary.

Every mark matters

If we want to make the most of a picture – to be open to it, and wonder why we feel as we do in front of it – we need to look not just at what is being represented but at everything that presents itself, grasping at the 'how' as well as the 'what'. Pictures are made of simple basic ingredients: arrangements of interwoven lines and shapes and colours, which the artist sets down in a particular medium and, at the same time, organizes. The movement of the pen or brush and the organizational decisions, made either consciously or unconsciously, and the medium itself induce an experience in the beholder. Finding the source of the experience does not diminish it in any way. Everything we see is affective, at times sets our hearts knocking and always sets our brains ticking.

Although picture-book art must be reproduced by a mechanical printing process, the print still records the technique used in the original and something of the effects of the chosen materials, even if the actual materiality is lost to our direct apprehension. As well as the materials, every mark, every modification of texture, the manner in which the pen or brush originally met the surface of the paper – delicately or boldly, incisively or sensuously – is telling.

Jane Hissey's crayon conjures the warm comforting feel of felt and fur and old worn carpeting for Little Bear's nursery because texture is perceived as a general quality of surface and therefore has strong associations with touch, which in turn has strong associations with our earliest infancy. As well,

12

"Where do you come from, Ted ?"

"From an idea," said Ted definitely.

"But ideas are not real, they are only made-up," said Teddy. "You have to come from somewhere real to have realitives."

"Not realitives, relatives!" said Ted trying to hide his confusion.

the medium itself – crayon – has cultural associations with childhood art.

Robert Ingpen's subtle colour modulations of the pastels he favours and their tactile quality can re-create the voluminous presence of a teddy bear   an idle bear – in a ruckled woolly jumper, just asking to be hugged.

The delicate, tremulous contour line in which John Burningham draws the little girl who gazes at her granpa's empty chair displays her feelings. Having made such a descriptive gesture in the quality of the line, Burningham does not need to put expression on her face if you 'know' what else to look for.

In *The True Story of the 3 Little Pigs* the expressive charge of the pictures is carried as much in the quality of the paint as in the objects represented. How the paint has been applied is in itself a metaphor for the wolf's energy and cunning, with every surface bubbling seething shifting scored and splattered, like the wily creature's ferocious energy, his protestations of innocence, and the layering of his lies.

Natural hues of earthy reds, umber and ochre help to realize the primitive world of the instincts.

Returning to the image of Ingpen's idle teddy bear, we can see that the ingredients from which he is made – line, colour, shape, texture, scale, separately and in combination – signify their own meaning and at the same time the representational meaning. You may look at the image piecemeal, enjoying the sweep of a curve for its own sake and attaching your personal associations to what you are looking at, but you can also admire the image as a whole and attach yet another set of associations; and at the same time where the line fades or sharpens or the tones lighten or darken, so you will 'read' the shape as a three-dimensional form with the bear's nose nearer to you than its ears; and at the same time, the pinks and blues of the jumper will make a lively contrast with the honey brown of the fur; and at the same time the powdery pastel plays its sensuous part, and all your private and cultural associations with bears and childhood will be attaching themselves. And the meaning of that picture will be in the sum total of the movements of the artist's hand as the medium was applied, the medium itself, and the organization of the ingredients.

It is not possible to attach significance solely to the formal elements or to the subject matter because the nature of that particular bear, including how near or far he is from you, *is* what he is made from. The point is that what the image represents, literally and expressively, is contained in everything you see.

Basic ingredients and composition

Pictures are made from simple basic ingredients, or abstract elements as they are sometimes called, and composition is the organization of these pictorial means. The easiest way to think about the basic ingredients at first is to concentrate on the design on the flat surface of the paper on which the picture is presented. The picture consists of several different kinds of interwoven arrangement –

- – a scheme of colour
- – a scheme of light and dark
- – a system of scale and intervals

14

- an arrangement of shapes
- an order of small- and large-scale patterning
- a network of linear rhythms.

The meaning of a figurative work of art, such as an illustration in a picture book, lies in the organization of these basic ingredients. When we look at a picture we perceive the ingredients and their organization as symbols referring to actual objects and (if we know how) to abstract notions.

Pictorial images and their modes of referring

Pictures have two basic modes of referring to things outside themselves: denotation and exemplification. Denotation is simple. A picture that represents an object refers to and denotes it. For example, a symbol of an apple denotes the fruit, apple. The meaning of the symbol is attached to the object. As long as you know what an apple is and how it is represented in your culture, you know what the symbol stands for: denotation doesn't depend upon truth to physical likeness. Think of Pat Hutchins's depiction of Rosie the hen, for example, and you immediately realize that animals in picture books do not necessarily bear literal resemblance to the real thing. Children are very familiar with denotation when they look at picture books, especially when they are being taught to read.

The other main mode of referring is called exemplification, which means that pictures show, by example, abstract notions, conditions, ideas, that cannot be pointed to directly but may be recognized through qualities or properties which the pictures literally or metaphorically display. Meanings do not come attached, as they do to symbols that denote. You have to select your meanings from a variety of possibilities and apply those which best suit the image(s) and the context.

The characteristic of the exemplifying symbol is its open nature; there is no single right answer. The different interpretations provoked by the penultimate and the final page openings of John Burningham's *Granpa* show that saying exactly what pictures exemplify is impossible. But we may welcome another interpretation if it is different from our own and find the work all the more interesting because we have several possibilities to choose from. Exemplifying

15

Outside Over There
© 1981
Maurice Sendak

Drawing upon the iconography of the Northern Romantic tradition, Sendak captures the atmosphere of a religious painting. Looming children, a visionary cloudscape, the paling moon, water, a rocky landscape, and a mysterious light source create a spiritual effect, which is further emphasized by Ida's pose and her blue dress.

symbols enable pictures to stand for something other than themselves: to function as art objects.

How exemplifying symbols are able to refer in this way becomes obvious if we think of specific examples from well-known picture books. In the page opening in Sendak's *Outside Over There* that shows the reunion of Ida and her baby sister, the latter is sitting in a broken eggshell, which on a literal level serves as a cradle. This is only made possible because Sendak has destroyed the natural relationship of scale between a human baby and an egg in the cause of super-natural reality. The child-chick's eggshell expresses the idea of innocence, rebirth, and plays a part in the quasi-religious symbolism of the composition as a whole, which in turn has its stylistic origins in the Northern Romantic tradition.

The pose of a depicted character is a dramatic, expressive gesture. We recognize a display of open hostility in the page opening in *Granpa* where the little girl and the old man have turned their backs on each other, and we are tempted to verbalize what each is thinking, feeling, and saying, from the facial expressions, poses, and the relationship between the position of each figure on the picture plane. An unworked expanse of white background is the metaphor for this rare moment of spiritual and physical isolation in a work which otherwise celebrates the closeness of the two characters. A pose may also signify a cultural association. Going back to the illustration of Ida, her kneeling figure in its blue dress, arms raised in joy and wonder at the sight of the baby before her, echoes the figure of the Virgin in Renaissance nativity paintings.

Settings and colour play expressive roles, and such is their importance in Deborah King's *Cloudy* that we can ascribe many different emotional atmospheres to the illustrations, as I try to show later. The abstract organization of a composition also acts as a visual metaphor. In *Outside Over There* Sendak is able to promote a dreamlike quality by using multiple viewpoints so that we may float about with Ida when she goes journeying. In *Where the Wild Things Are* Sendak chose to mirror the escalating scale of Max's psychological rage and rumpus by gradually increasing the size of the pictures in a succession of twelve page openings.

How exemplification – the object standing as an example of something outside itself – works is discussed in more detail in the close looking at Kitamura's *When Sheep Cannot Sleep* (pages 22-36).

A working vocabulary

Some useful terms, with brief definitions and examples, appear on pages 81 to 94.

Close Looking in Context

In this section I briefly describe my approach, which I hope will put close looking in the context of reading a picture book as a whole. The actual experience is not so neatly compartmentalized as my account of it, but everything that is described does happen.

Picking up a picture book I am aware of its size and shape in my hands as I read the title, glance at the cover illustration, and note the names of the author and the artist. If I already know the work of either, in rush expectations and assumptions, which it might be better not to have at this stage but which are inevitable.

The first time through, I am faced with the uniqueness of the picture-book form itself. I have a compelling curiosity to read on to find out what happens next, but this works against the pictures, which would have me stop and search. The immediate tension is resolved by skimming words and images to get a general idea of what the book is about and what I might make from it, but no more than that. Then I'll skim it all over again.

The third time through I read the words and look at the pictures much more slowly, to begin the process of discovering what relationship(s) they have. There is a range of possibilities, some much more obvious than others. The pictures may elaborate, amplify, extend, and complement the words. Or the pictures may appear to contradict or 'deviate' in feeling from what the words imply. A variant of this happens when the words and pictures counterpoint each other so that two separate stories run in tandem, as in John Burningham's *Shirley* books. Picture-book art favours 'running stories' in addition to the main one, so we have to observe small pictorial details as well as what the words say in order to 'get the whole picture'. The emotional tone of the composite text emerges from the interaction of the two sources of information – words that tell and pictures that show.

As I go through the picture book I keep an open mind. For the moment, there will be plenty of feelings in response to the text and illustrations, and I shall have been given more

18

information than I know how to handle, so the thing to do next is to stand back from the book as a whole, and go into the pictures in a systematic way.

Now begins the close looking, and the sections on *When Sheep Cannot Sleep* and *Cloudy* describe the process. I cannot know how much time I shall need, what I shall find, what I can make. Close looking cannot be hurried; the term 'beholder' is particularly appropriate to the action since it implies staying put and holding on to what is being given until it has had time to work upon you and you upon it. Although I am concentrating upon the images, what I already know about the facts of the story will affect my interpretation – how can they not? Even the title of a textless picture book has its say.

Then on to the text in a systematic way as well, reading it page by page, and looking at the pictures, switching from one to the other, noticing whether the text runs on in front of the pictures, hinting at what will happen, or whether it is saying broadly what the pictures show specifically or whether words and pictures appear to be having different lives of their own. This gives me a fresh perspective on the depicted objects and settings.

Quite often I will copy out the text, line by line to reproduce the pattern of how the words are arranged on the page, and I doublespace my copy to indicate each turn of the page. This concentrates my attention upon the language alone – its rhythms and word order and tone. I will also make two columns, and write the text in its page segments on one side, and describe the main features of the picture on the other so that what's being told may be compared with what's being shown. And this activity will highlight what the beholder has to contribute in the time-and-space of the turn of the page, which is a major feature of the picture-book form.

At this stage I will be recognizing recurrent motifs, devices like whether colour is being used naturalistically or for emotional effect, and all the time I will be trying to make relationships between the objects themselves and their appearances on previous and succeeding pages, and relationships between the pictured world and the themes it explores. (Associations here may send me researching styles, historical periods, and to histories of ideas.)

19

I look at the pattern of text and illustration in combination, and if there are textless page openings I will be asking myself what effect these have on the rhythms of the story. Am I being hurried along or slowed down? And all the time I am rereading the text, dipping between the openings, searching the pictures, and making tiny notes about anything and everything which seem to jump out at me.

At some stage, when I think I have noticed everything, I pull it all together – words, pictures, the object itself – and ask myself what this art object expresses, and exemplifies, and what values it is promoting. When I reread that same picture book later, often I will find many more features I've overlooked, and so the hypothesizing and interpretation and evaluation continue until the covers close once more.

As a final observation, not all picture books will keep you engaged in the same way at all stages because there is such variety of style and form. At one extreme is the picture book that is highly expressive and explores interesting themes, while at the other extreme is the picture book that is really a game in hard covers. Both may be enjoyed equally but differently. Sometimes there will be much to be made from the structure of the compositions, as in Jane Ray's *The Story of Christmas*. With other picture books there could be features of style that invite placing in a historical or cultural framework, such as Sendak's *Outside Over There*. A picture book may be very painterly – *The Whales' Song*, for instance – offering a sensuous experience through obvious effects of texture and colour; or predominantly graphic, like the works of Fiona French: varied in approach to suit the text, always controlled, decorative, elegant, inventive. Another may be full of closely observed social practices presented as visual jokes, as in *I Hate My Teddy Bear* by David McKee. *The Jolly Postman* by Janet and Allan Ahlberg plays with literary conventions and contemporary phenomena, and lets us read other people's mail with a clear conscience. *The True Story of the 3 Little Pigs* by Scieszka and Smith is painterly, and literary, and highly ironic in showing, telling, and what happens between the two systems. *Strat and Chatto* with words by Jan Mark and pictures by David Hughes invites you to see what may be accomplished by line and a lineage stretching back to nineteenth-century cartoons as well as being something of a fable for our times.

Whatever the form and style of a particular picture book, it is there for us to make something positive from it for ourselves.

This account of 'close looking in context' is my definition of an aesthetic experience. When we hold a picture book, we have in our hands a pictured world full of ideas. We play with these ideas and play our own ideas around the pictured world. The more skilful we are, and the more ideas the picture book contains, the more the ideas go on bouncing. And in the process we create something of our very own.

Close Looking in Action

When Sheep Cannot Sleep and Cloudy

I have chosen two picture books for young children to illustrate some of the factors involved in close looking at pictures. At first viewing there doesn't appear to be a great deal going on in either book, the Kitamura with its direct visual narrative and King's immediately accessible pictures: no visual punnings, or games, or sophisticated counterpointing between words and images – those distinctive features of some other artists' work about which it is easy to find things to say. This straightforwardness is so much the better because it leaves us free to concentrate on:

- how the lines, shapes and colours have been set down and organized
- the choice of medium and its effect
- what is being shown both literally and expressively.

I have treated the two picture books slightly differently. With *When Sheep Cannot Sleep* I have concentrated on line and linear emphases, colour and contrasts of tone, shapes, viewpoint, patterning, as well as how pictorial symbols are able to exemplify. With *Cloudy* the close reading broadens to include the relationship of words and images, the effect of the pictures and typography, and the physical format of the book itself.

It will be helpful if you number the pages of the books in page-opening units (also called doublespreads), starting with the picture that accompanies the beginning of the text.

Looking at Woolly

When Sheep Cannot Sleep is an art object since it is expressive, and it also deals with the concept of number. An adventure story accompanied by expressive pictures gives form to ideas about the nature of creativity. At the same time, the pictures, one after the other, display increasing numbers of interesting objects which the beholder might like to count, although there are no direct instructions to do so.

The story is told with unforced humour and in childlike vocabulary, speech patterns and tone. Woolly the Sheep goes on his insomniac rambles in the gathering dusk and under a luminous night sky. He observes first a butterfly, then two ladybirds, hears three owls *hoo-hoo-hoo*, sees bats above his head and grasshoppers under his hooves, and so on, until he comes upon a mysterious empty house. He occupies himself within the house until, finally exhausted by his adventures, he falls asleep counting his relatives.

The layout is simple. Nothing distracts from the orderly sequence of three-quarter plates, beneath each of which is set a brief portion of the text in double line spacing. There is an airiness about the generous proportion of wide white margin which frames the richly coloured paintings. Woolly himself is an endearing creature with a sagacious look, a thoroughly credible being.

With any picture book, when I arrive at the close-looking stage, I have already gone through the book several times and have gathered many impressions. The systematic search for the origins of these impressions always begins with looking at lines of all kinds. The line gets me closest to the artist, which is where I want to be at this stage. The drawn (or painted) line is a direct record of the movement of the artist's hand, describing objects and events. The line that tells you about the pictured world reveals at the same time something of the personality of the picture-maker and how he thinks and feels about what he is doing. Does this have an effect upon the viewer? Surely it must. The emotional experience of looking at a picture book illustrated by Satoshi Kitamura or Charles Keeping or Quentin Blake is different in each case, and the quality of the artist's line is a major shaping force.

Line

Line creates contour, modelling, shading and a sign for movement. A contour puts a line round objects and figures and gives them their individuality and character. Page opening 8, left, where Woolly is shown in the hall of the empty house, is characteristic of Kitamura's style. He prefers to do as little underdrawing as possible, therefore his pen meets the paper once and for all, with no margin for error, no chance to reconsider. The quality of the line is fine,

unbroken, and exhibits a slight tremor, which charges the drawing with energy. It is as if the concentration required to get the line down just as he wanted it is still present in the contour.

When Kitamura defines objects he uses a closed contour line, precisely filled with colour. A closed contour contains an object and separates it totally from its surroundings. This

24

mode of drawing attention to an object suits Kitamura's purpose well, since many of his objects have specific symbolic as well as narrative functions and thus reward close attention, and often he is concerned to promote a surreal effect by the juxtaposition of unlikely objects, to suggest his characters' inner lives. For example, the open door is a recurrent motif in Woolly's story, and interpreting that is a little puzzle for the beholder. (There are numerous other examples in Kitamura's picture books. In *Ned and the Joybaloo* Kitamura signals the protagonist's freedom from a world dictated by geographical limitations, gravity, and time with three homely objects – a globe, an apple, an egg timer – which fly into the air as Ned bursts into an imaginary dimension.)

If he used the continuous line and colour alone, Kitamura would have no way of softening the passage from the shape of one object to another, no way of suggesting the relativity of existence or the connections between objects. To some extent he resolves this problem by using water-soluble black inks in his pens: one ink with a sepia trace, the other blue. When he has drawn his images, he applies a plain water wash over selected areas, which causes the ink to 'run' and thus modulate the precise definitions of the line. These passages with their insidious colour and tonal shifts and drifts have a unifying effect on the composition as a whole. The tension between the tightly controlled line and the escaping watery staining gives the picture much of its sense of vitality and is particularly effective in the otherwise rigid structure and static composition of Woolly and the twelve trompe l'oeil doors (page opening 8, left).

In drawing, lines are also used to create tone (light and dark) which models form (solid shape). In this case, the lines are used inside the contour for modelling, to imitate the effect of light on a form. And since the illusion of a three-dimensional world depends upon relating the forms each to the other in space, line is used between the forms to render the effects of lighting conditions – for example, to suggest shadowy depths.

Tone is more fully discussed in the section on colour (pages 30-31), but I need to mention it here because 'line and wash', or drawing coloured in transparent paints or inks, is a very popular medium in picture books: the three-dimensional effects in illustrations are often created by lines in conjunction with colour. The presence of lines affects the tone of the colour. Imagine an area of lightish green paint. Lines drawn on this area will lower the tone of (appear to darken) the green and cause it to recede.

Line may also be used to indicate the direction of a particular plane or the internal form of a shape by bracelet shading as on human limbs or tree trunks. And through the use of lines of different weight and thickness, line suggests movement. Examples of all these uses of line may be found on page opening 7.

Taking the left plate first, we can see that texturing lowers the tone of a surface, and so although the grassy track over which Woolly runs 'as fast as he could' is light green in colour, dense irregular hatching settles it back into the middle plane of the picture. The lines are of varying weight, which gives them an organic quality, while the direction in which they lie, as if the grass is being blown from right to left, like the row of tulips, implies movement. As Woolly's form canters in from left to right and goes downhill, there is a tremendous kinetic energy arising from the contrast between the lie of the patterned grass and flowers and his pure white shape. Minimal bracelet shading gives volume to the tree trunks. Scratchy hatchings and crosshatchings denote the density of foliage on the trees as well as something of the planes on which the foliage lies.

On the opposing plate, which shows Woolly in a field before a house, the very absence of lines of texture has a special effect. Woolly stands at the left of the composition, asking, 'Where am I?' The foreground to the left is textured with scratches to indicate grass, which lead in to the right, the direction in which the house is sited. In contrast, over at the right, the field area is not only paler and lighter in tone but also unworked. If we then consider the angle from which the house is shown, we see that the viewpoint is from over on the right; that is, not from Woolly's point of view but from someone standing opposite him on the light-toned empty area. There is an implied spectator sharing the view within Woolly's world, someone to whom he addresses his question. The picture-book beholder has joined the night's adventure.

Linear emphases

As well as the visible lines made by the artist's pen or brush, we often see linear emphases as a result of the patterning of shapes, contrasts, similarities of colours and so on, and these emphases are analogous to psychological states. Some of the individual elements in a composition may be static and give repose and stability while others may be dynamic and make for motion or instability.

We respond through how we feel and know the world to be. For example, horizontal and vertical emphases suggest stability because we associate the feel of the solid ground beneath our feet, the sight of a figure standing upright and confident, or what we know of good solid building, with the anchoring effect of gravitational pull. A very different visual rhythm is set up by waving patterns which promote the feel of continuous and smooth movement as in wind rippling long grass or a gentle swell at sea. A triangular emphasis in a composition 'speaks' of serenity, endurance and a range of associations arising from the combination of earth-boundness and aspiring height. But invert that shape or tip a triangle and feel the elements move.

Page opening 6, right plate, which shows Woolly at the top of a hill, feeling scared at the sight of a squadron of UFOs, makes the point. The rising diagonals of the line of flying saucers and the descending diagonal of the hillside, together with the right side of the frame of the illustration, create an isosceles triangle turned through forty-five degrees. Woolly appears to be poised on the very edge of disaster. Will he topple? The effect is emphasized by the apple core he has dropped, which is fast falling into the mysterious deep blue depths of the abyss in front of his hooves. Diagonals are always associated with off-balance, and an emphasis from lower left to upper right will be understood as rising, as energy, going up in the world, friction, while the reverse direction is felt as falling, literally and metaphorically.

To the explanation above – that we read movement or repose in the linear emphases through analogies and psychological suggestions – might be added the optical and perceptual theories of Rudolf Arnheim, about the various effects created by an object's position relative to the square or rectangle on which it is placed. He says that perceptual forces

Rudolf Arnheim
Art and Visual Perception
Univ. California Press
1974

cause us to see pushes and pulls in visual patterns as genuine properties of the perceived objects themselves. These perceptual forces are strongest at the centre of a picture, with strong pulls to each corner, and other pulls to the centre of each side. By drawing the vertical and horizontal axes, and the diagonals, over a rectangular or square picture, you can make apparent the invisible lines on which the forces lie.

Looking at a picture in this way invites the beholder to consider how the elements are held in balance so that they create the psychological and perceptual effect desired by the artist. Weight is a factor that determines balance, so we are now considering shapes and colours and patterns as having perceptual weight.

Various factors affect weight, according to Arnheim. An object in the upper part of a composition is perceived as heavier than one in the lower. Location on the right side of the picture makes for more weight than location on the left. Weight also depends on size: larger objects will be heavier than small ones. Bright colours are heavier than dark ones. Isolation is a means of emphasis, and circular shapes too, and an isolated circle counterweighs a larger rectangle and triangle. Regular shapes are heavier than irregular ones. And (despite what the artist intends) weight may depend upon the intrinsic interest of the beholder or upon the beholder's wishes and fears.

Some of these factors may be demonstrated through looking at the plate which shows Woolly in the hall of the empty house (page opening 8, left plate). A structural map shows that the centre of the picture lies just below and to the left of the open door. Woolly is a bright white isolated shape in the lower half of the picture. His face and round eyes to the left of the centre line balance the door which lies to the right in the upper half of the picture. The weight of the dark, warm, red carpet is sufficiently strong to counterbalance the much larger area of the cool greys of the walls and ceilings.

Although Woolly is on a relatively small scale in the picture as a whole, our intrinsic interest in the sheep ensures that he is a weighty object and, in relation to the red of the carpet either side of him, he is in a comfortably large scale. It depends which part of the picture we take to be the background for his figure. The effect of the two scales (the sets of intervals between Woolly and his immediate

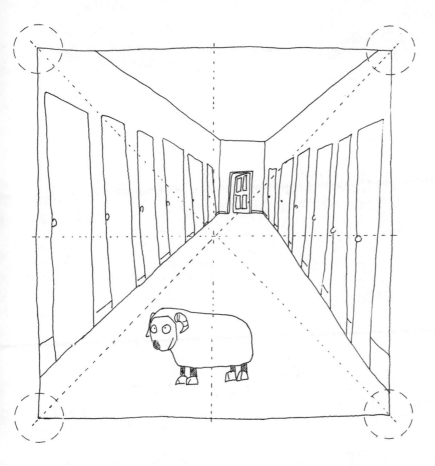

From **When Sheep Cannot Sleep**
See reproduction on page 24

*The dotted lines represent what Arnheim calls the 'structural
skeleton' of the square (these skeletons vary, depending on the
figure). Wherever a pictured object is located, it will be affected by
the forces of all the hidden structural factors. The open door lies near
the perceptual centre of the picture, which is always a little above the
physical centre. The pulls to each of the corners act upon the
diagonal lines of floor and ceiling. Because these lines do not come
to rest in the corners themselves, they imply that the fourth wall of
the hall lies 'in front of' the picture plane – giving us space in which
to view the scene. If you stand the picture book on its lower edge and
look at this particular composition in the vertical (as if it were a
picture on a wall), the hallway looks longer, and the far doorway
even more of a lure, than if you hold the book tilted in your hands.*

background, and Woolly and the picture plane) creates tension: he is small and vulnerable and yet not overwhelmed. Kitamura's organization here is very subtle.

I cannot be sure, of course, how much of these interpretations about movement and balance depend upon analogies and psychological suggestions, and how much I owe to optical and perceptual factors. They seem to act as one.

Picture-book illustrations designed in irregular shapes to accommodate the literary content of the story will not have the classical balance of those that are paintings in the conventional sense. With all types of picture-book illustration, however, it is often interesting to treat the whole page (or, if appropriate, the doublespread) as if it were a picture plane and see where objects are disposed, or where the illustration lies in relation to the edges of the paper. Such factors affect our reception of the picture and the possibilities for interpretation.

Colour

There are three terms which correspond to the way in which the eye sorts and sees colour. Knowing these terms refines the ways we can express ourselves when talking about colour effects. A colour has

- hue
- tone
- saturation.

Hue is the term used to distinguish the colours that range from one end of the spectrum to the other. When we call a colour 'blue', we refer to its hue. There are about 150 discernible hues, and attempting to name them all would be a neat way of demonstrating the difficulties of being verbally precise about visual signs. For an artist, hue refers to the name of a pigment.

Tone is a measure of light and dark of an area regardless of its colour, and is the quality of a surface as measured purely by its position in the scale between black and white. Tone imitates the effect of light on a form and may be distinguished from hue (looking at colour through half-closed eyes helps you to distinguish tonal values). Tone (shading) is used to model an object, showing us its physical structure, giving us the equivalent of what it would feel like if we could hold that object and know it through the pads of our fingers and the palms of our hands. Tone renders the effects of texture (a heavy texture like tree foliage will tend to be darker than lighter textured grass). Tone also renders the effect of lighting and weather conditions across a whole picture.

Light and dark not only represent lighting effects but also have symbolic and emotional associations for us. A high-key colour scheme using light colours is able to suggest feelings of well-being, whereas a low-key scheme in dark colours may well have a more sombre effect.

Saturation is the measure of the purity of a colour. Red, yellow and blue (the primary colours) are pigments with the highest level of intensity or saturation, and yellow is the brightest of the three. As a pigment, white is also a saturated colour. All these colours could be described as 'strong', 'pure', 'fully saturated'. Colours with little saturation are greyish. A neutral grey would be described as 'dull', 'unsaturated'. Emotional connotations are communicated more strongly by tone and saturation than by hue, with the exception of the link between red and warmth, according to a study cited by Nodelman (see 'On The Bookshelf', page 79), a theory we will now put to the test.

If we slowly turn the pages of *When Sheep Cannot Sleep* and look at the entire sequence of illustrations as a set of two-dimensional patterns of lightness and darkness, a visual rhythm emerges. In the first fourteen plates, in almost every case, there are bands of dark tones in the upper half contrasted by light tones in the lower half. In the fifteenth illlustration, where Woolly is depicted doing some drawing, light tones dominate the whole plane. The pattern is reversed thereafter, with light tones above and dark tones beneath, except where Woolly begins to think as he lies in bed, where dark tones dominate the whole plane.

Dark light . . . dark light . . . light . . . light dark . . . light dark . . . dark . . . light dark. Easy as a lullaby. What's to be made from the pattern? The first pictures show Woolly adventuring in the countryside and in the hall of the empty house. The later pictures show Woolly in action all over the house before he finally falls asleep. In the illustration that has the light background Woolly engages in work which is also a creative

31

act. As one student said, 'Here Woolly is in charge of the darkness.' Indeed he is.

See reproduction of the 'Woolly at work' illustration opposite title page

Woolly at work is a hinge illustration. Before it, he is something of a sheep, but at work and thereafter he is very much a child in sheep's clothing. The composition is simple, the details few, so let us stop there and consider what's involved in interpreting just one picture: what we are given, what we perceive, how we construct our various meanings.

We perceive Woolly drawing in an otherwise empty room, we read the text below, we remember, we project, we make relationships. But if we pause here and look at the abstract elements and the composition, what might we make of them?

I have already referred to the generous space of white margin which surrounds the coloured plate and accommodates the text and which in its cumulative effect contributes to the quiet formality of the whole book. Like all the illustrations, the plate is framed in a finely drawn free-hand line. The frame has an organic quality, as if it is expanding and contracting very very gently against the life of the pictured world, as well as being of a piece with the quality of the drawing within it. The background colours are slightly warm, pink and yellow ochre, and have a lightish tone and a lowish intensity. They promote a serene quality. This large homogeneous area is contrasted with a medium area of darker tone – a variety of browns which makes up the desk and the cast shadow. The crayons, the colours of the rainbow and the saturated yellow the brightest of all, contrast in scale with the desk top and Woolly's drawing paper.

There is another play-off of contrast of plain and patterning between the planked floor and the undecorated wall. Although the yellow ochre flooring is a larger area than the pink wall, the wall carries more weight, being in the upper part of the picture, and can balance the flooring.

A narrow horizontal band of white (the skirting board) runs in from both sides of the far plane to focus attention on both Woolly and the open door through which he's come. This band also arrests the slightly diagonal flow of the blocks of regular shapes (floorboards) with which Kitamura creates the illusion of space. Woolly's head and upper torso make a strong white triangular shape in a composition which has many horizontal emphases: wall, floor, drawing paper, desk

32

and its shadow, and skirting board. He is placed a little above the centre of the picture plane, with symmetry of space between his form and either side of the outer edges of the picture, further symmetry of design being offered through the shapes of desk and shadow.

Within this composition the balance of lightness, spaciousness and stability exemplifies tranquillity and freedom from distraction. And as one of a series of pictures, the serene room contrasts with the darkening skies of the preceding pictures, and the dark floors of the pictures that follow. Here is the psychological high point of Woolly's tale.

If we move on to consider the depicted objects as symbols, Woolly, the sheep as an artist, will have personal associations for the beholder, conscious and possibly subconscious, but we may well share many of the meanings which are mentioned.

On the simple denotational level, there is Woolly as himself, drawing at a desk in an empty room, with a glimpse of the hallway through the open door.

On the level of exemplification and expression, Woolly will also stand for abstract notions in relation to the themes of this text; he will stand for cultural and societal values; he allows for intertextual references. Colour and tonal conventions will affect meanings. For example, Woolly as a narrowly disguised human being belongs to the very old anthropomorphic tradition. Did not Aesop use animals to point moral lessons about human behaviour? Woolly is also an example of the folklore of how to woo sleep. He refers to a particular kind of artistic activity: drawing. At the same time he is engaged in what we all do − telling stories to himself about himself in order to make sense of what is happening. Being a Kitamura hero, his stories take pictorial form. Woolly is a model of good behaviour, being able to entertain himself in solitude. Of course, he is an example of this particular artist's oeuvre, taking his place with all the other independent, creative, resourceful Kitamura protagonists. And he defies stereotyping in that he is not in the least silly. Finally, Woolly at work is a sophisticated comment on the value of art and creativity.

And what do you make of the door? The open door is a recurrent motif ... we are told that the front door of the house was open, and interior doors are depicted likewise. Do

33

you see the open door as a symbol for the passage of time and space as Woolly passes from one part of the house to another, or as rather a threatening element? Woolly is always in a vulnerable position with his back to it. Or maybe you see it as an example of the way children behave, never shutting doors behind them. All three interpretations have been voiced by students studying this picture book with me.

Shapes, viewpoint, patterning

The last picture to be discussed, of Woolly in the kitchen preparing his supper (page opening 9, left), makes a striking contrast to the portrait of the artist as a young sheep, and will help to illustrate the importance of viewpoint, as well as how the character of a composition is controlled fundamentally by the regularity or irregularity of the various sizes of shapes. A word about the character of the shapes themselves first.

The shapes of Kitamura's forms are sculptural, simplified, and tend towards the angular, with scant concern for anatomy or the rules of projective realism. Kitamura often gives two viewpoints on individual objects; we may look at a tin of peas at almost eye level, the better to read its label and observe how solidly it sits upon a surface, but in addition we may also look down on it from above, the better to enjoy its contents. The effect of the second viewpoint is to tilt the upper surface towards us, and to make the total form more accessible. This is how we 'know' a jar by both looking at and handling it.

With this talk of viewpoints, here is an appropriate place to mention perspective – the way an artist controls space in a picture. There are many kinds of perspective, and the optical system at its most extreme with its fixed viewpoint, which was formalized in the Renaissance, is never rigidly applied in picture-book illustrations. Picture-book narrative is often concerned with action so it's not surprising that an artist will prefer to use more than one eye level within a single picture, or to send us travelling along the picture by multiple viewpoints at a fixed level.

The most important function of whatever system of perspective is applied, is to establish the viewpoint of the beholder in relation to the picture. Is the artist inviting us to look up to, or to look down upon the subject matter; or to

34

look it in the eye? This has a marked psychological effect upon how we relate to what we are looking at. For example, Kitamura favours high viewpoints in the latter part of *When Sheep Cannot Sleep*, which makes Woolly appear something like a child at play from our point of view. Here he is alone in the empty house, being very busy and resourceful, and yet he is particularly endearing, just as a small child is, when

When Sheep Cannot Sleep
© *1986 Satoshi Kitamura*

mimicking adult activities. In contrast, the low eye level in an earlier painting (page opening 6, right) brings us down in the dense grass with Woolly amongst the singing grasshoppers.

Back to the kitchen. The composition has a series of powerful diagonal emphases and a high viewpoint. Kitamura has chosen an arrangement much favoured in Japanese art, having its origins in the paintings on screens. Such solutions coupled with Western imagery give his style a strong individual identity. We are literally looking down on Woolly, and in this instance a child beholder might be amused by and feel rather superior to a chef who cooks peas in a frying pan.

The runaway lines of floor, table top, skirting, sink unit and cooker top and shelf, are arrested by the vertical emphases on the right-hand side created by the flowers, cup, stool, coffee filter, and toaster. There are many small objects to the left on the draining board – bottles, mill, tins, cartons – which create small vertical emphases, as well as balance the fewer, larger objects which they oppose. There is contrast of shapes: in the lower foreground patterns of small irregular circles signifying tin tops, plates, rings, pan, pots vie with the regular squares of the two-tone blue tiled floor in the upper background. The character of the composition is busy, and at its busiest in the foreground – the area between the sheep and the beholder. The homely clutter surrounding Woolly, the stir of shapes and colours and lines, is offset by only one area which is plain: the wall by the door, the door which is coming to be associated with the little sheep.

As for the picture book as a whole, literal exemplification gives us a time scale from evening to night, and in itself the sequence of numbers implies time, and simultaneously, as we read and count, the story goes forward through the countryside and through the house, as does the notion of numeracy. Metaphorically, the book exemplifies time as experienced by a child at play – time to do this, and then time to do that – which the tone of the text underlines. Satoshi Kitamura is a picture-book artist whose work can serve a practical function, like giving an opportunity to practise number, as well as offer his beholders an affective and aesthetic experience.

36

Looking at Cloudy

The informed looking-process continues with Deborah King's *Cloudy* and includes attention to the verbal text. *Cloudy* is not only a story about a cat but stories about the art of manipulation and mood setting. One good reason for choosing this picture book is that young children love it and respond to it with 'peaceful concentration and respect'. As one infant teacher put it:

> This is one of those complete experiences that enriches the reader – with language, colour, texture, feelings – a glimpse of life that isn't diminished by being repeated over and over.

But *Cloudy* is also able to prove the point that there is no such thing as a picture book that is too young for the reader if that reader has been trained to use his or her eyes and ask pertinent questions.

Picture book as object

Cloudy pictures a country cat's secret life, a life that doesn't directly include humans. In a series of doublespreads (or page openings) we enter Cloudy's territory, not always as observers, for in several openings Deborah King gives us a sufficiently muscular experience to enable us to come close to feeling 'what it is like to be' the cat herself.

Beginning with the shape of the book itself, the landscape format carries its own expressive charge: *Cloudy* is much wider than it is high, an emphasis that suits a tale about journeying through the landscape, the times of day, the changes of weather, and encourages empathy with such actions as a leap to kill or a sensuous stretch in the dust. Normally in a series of illustrations containing many objects and details, the settings would encourage detachment as we look at all the clues we are being given, working on the assumption that, in art as in life, appearances are telling. In this picture book, though, we not only interpret Cloudy's interior characteristics in terms of her setting but are also encouraged by the artist to share her space.

Layout

King uses doublespreads which bleed on all four sides so that Cloudy's world has no beginning or end, being without boundaries and somewhat panoramic for the spectator.

Text

The text makes a series of undecorated statements. On the first opening Cloudy introduces herself:

> I am a little grey cat called Cloudy.
> I am the colour of thunder and rain.
> It's difficult to see me on dull days.

After this, almost to the end, the text is a single sentence, describing a single action, which the picture shows apparently simply and directly. Cloudy is blown by the wind. She lurks in tumbledown sheds. She hunts. She sits by the fire. She prowls. On the penultimate spread, as Cloudy eases

Cloudy
© 1989 Deborah King

...when I disappear again.

herself through a cat flap, the text stretches beyond a single sentence by three words continuing over the next opening, which shows the cat asleep on a sofa beside a dog (an intertextual reference to *Jake* by the same artist) and continues overleaf again, to conclude on the final plate. Here, in the first light of dawn, Cloudy is shown leading us off again, a small image looking back over her shoulder. Are you coming? Thus the climax is but a sleep and a stretch at the conclusion of the book, and an invitation to make a new beginning.

The narrative thrust is minimal, which is unusual in a picture book, where often curiosity about how the story will develop is what drives the reader on, working against the pictures, which by their nature would have the beholder stay. But the story line in *Cloudy* provides only a skeletal framework for the pictures, which are rich in creative moods. This is not to say that the text is virtually superfluous. There is an intermittent play-off between words and pictures as Cloudy insists on telling us how difficult she is to see, how she can disappear in long grass, in dust and shadows, invisible in moonlight or early morning or beside the fire. But of course we can see her because we have been let into her secret life, so there is a simple ironic counterpoint between what she believes and what we know.

As a device counterpoint usually requires the reader to take an objective stance: when the pictures are showing a different account of what the words are saying, we aren't meant to take the words at face value. But rather than feeling pleased with ourselves at being able to arrive at a truth which lies between the words and the images, the effect in *Cloudy* is to increase the sense of partnership and empathy with the little cat through a gentle joke. We can see her, but with us she is safe, of course.

Typography

The text appears to be printed in grey (an effect achieved by laying a mechanical tint over the solid black lettering) and subtly supports Cloudy's assertions about her elusiveness and allows the illustrations to be the focus of attention. The tone of the grey varies from chalky to graphite according to the hue and tone of the background and the mood of the action being described. The text 'runs like the wind' in lightest alphabet letters, but 'hunts' in a darker, deadlier strength. Thus the visual weight of the printed words has a marked rhythm, while at the same time their integration with the picture surface is as complete as possible. This is an important feature in a set of illustrations attempting to create the illusion of the reality of the pictured world, for the artist would have us believe that what we are looking at has three dimensions. Inevitably, lettering is perceived in two dimensions, so that its presence superimposed on a picture always threatens the illusion of depth. King has solved this problem to a considerable extent.

Colour

Colour is pressed into double service. It both creates a convincing physical world and, at the same time, suggests various moods while remaining true to a palette of natural hues. Colour is a way of seeing. In the actual world the sensation in our field of vision that we call colour enables us to distinguish between one object and another, it informs us about chemical and physical structure, about texture or weather or light (Gore, see reference, page 5). With symbolic and emotional interpretation, we 'read into' colour much as we read into texts, and what we see depends upon facts of the natural world, individual and cultural associations, personal colour sense.

The same colour may display friendly or disturbing aspects according to context. Consider the tall spears of grass in which Cloudy roams at dusk (page opening 10). Painted in a range of red ochres that would serve equally well to suggest autumnal beauty and sunset on downlands, these naturalistic associations are not the only ones that come to mind. We are also being shown a tooth-and-claw background, stained in symbolic red-for-danger. All the qualities of colour, including how it is applied – the relative opacity or translucency, intensity, dullness, darkness or lightness, the cool or warm effects – contribute to symbolic meaning. In *Cloudy*, for example, grey – the colour of the cat and the clouds – is particularly important.

In the first presentation of the heroine, on the cover, her golden eyes dominate a large-scale head-and-shoulders

40

portrait: a feline icon. The viewer's eye level and the cat's are the same, so the effect is that of coming face to face with her in the long golden grasses, with the wild grey sky above. The cat's fur is built up in delicate brushwork, with meticulous modulations of tone and with a density that gives the impression of her physical presence and volume. In contrast, the sky is painted in loose, translucent washes, forms with outlines that seem to dissolve and shift as we watch them.

See reproduction of the Cloudy *front cover on page 6*

The invitation to identify Cloudy with the skyscape is sent through the colour since they share the same hue and tones; the quality of the medium and the way the clouds are painted present the idea of something that cannot be held down – a visual metaphor for the elusive essence shared by the clouds and this creature. The association is reinforced by skyscapes of motley clouds on the half title, dedication and copyright, and title pages; by grey endpapers and cloudy-grey print.

As well as a range of greys, other dominant hues are ochres and earth-red, pigments that could be dug from the very landscape itself. Golden ochre, by surface pattern and symbol, links the cat to the territory she inhabits, the importance of which is established on the cover itself.

King uses contrasts and closeness of tones very effectively. In the first doublespread, for example, she depicts Cloudy in the wide open downlands under a grey sky. Although the grasses are gold and green and the little cat is grey, so close are the tones that the animal is 'difficult to see' just as she claims to be in the text. On the other hand, the contrast between the darker tones of the countryside and the lighter tones of the sky emphasizes the linearity of the composition and the effect of wide-open space. The low eye level introduced on the cover is still held as we sneak into the tale and watch the cat on the extreme right, relatively small now, padding off in a rhythmic stride, tail erect, luring us to follow.

Pictorial analogies and exemplification

If we stay with this composition for just a moment, it will serve to illustrate what might be called pictorial analogies*

---

*Frederick Gore quotes Delacroix as saying that composition is 'the organization of analogies'. Gore calls these 'plastic analogies'. I have changed the term, but owe to Gore the description of what the idea encompasses.

41

I am a little grey cat called Cloudy.
I am the colour of thunder and rain.
It's difficult to see me on dull days.

Cloudy
© *1989 Deborah King*

and how they serve exemplification. Pictorial analogies are the metaphors and similes of painting which enable what is shown to appear as one thing but also to carry other meanings.

To discover pictorial analogies, look for the abstract repetition of shapes and lines, of proportions and patterns in the scheme, as well as at what they represent. In the previous section I have written about colour and the linearity of the composition tonally. There are also repetitions of shapes and lines that give further power through the affinities they make between animate and inanimate objects. The horizon is as sinuous, as gently curved, as the cat's back. Her whiskers are miniature threads of the grasses in form, tone and colour. Horizontal streaks of light break the clouds in the background just as Cloudy's tail in the foreground breaks our view of the horizon. The angle at which her ears are set is continued in a fold of the far hillside. The movement of the clouds, the movement of the landscape continue the movement of the figure.

The formal links supply a psychological link: the cat's temperament as well as her grace is fully displayed in a composition which literally and metaphorically shows her to be at one with nature.

*

42

Scale

Hereafter we shall see Cloudy in alternating large and small scale. The large-scale close-ups modify the relationship between cat and viewer (page opening 2); this is what it is like to be rolling in the dirt – King shows a huge image of the cat, eyes closed in ecstasy, in a mosaic of dust clouds and part-forms of furry limbs, stretching across the doublespread. When Cloudy is hunting out in the wilds (page opening 10), the beholder is taken by surprise within a whisker of her nose. When she is depicted in small scale, the compositional arrangement and the colour schemes enable us to share the emotional and physical atmosphere. When she tells us that she is but 'a ball of fluff' when the wind blows, we see her, head dropped and her back set against the elements. The wild wind scouring the downlands flattens the grass, transforms the bare trees to whips, their branches to lashing thongs. The horizon vanishes as cloudscape and landscape merge, both treated in the same bleached hues; imagine the colour of wind if you can. What-it-feels-like-in-the-presence-of-a-gale is the metaphorical subject of the picture.

Elsewhere, Cloudy is portrayed sleeping, in small scale, in two interiors – stable and kitchen – both compositions painted in dark warm harmonious hues of copper, umber, a range of smoky greys, violety black, and a tranquil green which edges to indigo. Textured patterning covers the entire surface of the picture plane, by stroke, dab, dot, and touch, giving it a furry quality. The effect of these two paintings is the visual equivalent of a purr.

Rhythms

To the physical rhythms – of prowl, leap and sleep, and the broad graphic rhythms of pictures in which predominantly light and dark tones take turn; of alternating close-up and far view; and of a lettering which varies in weight – may be added the rhythm belonging to the life of the cat herself. Although we see Cloudy at various points in her life, times of the day and night, and seasons, the chronology is not a simple linear progression. Several years or less than an hour may pass in the turning of a page, as naturally and easily as a succession of thoughts passes through a recollective mind.

43

Furthermore, and of crucial bearing in these paintings, is a rhythmic patterning as King sharpens or leaves undefined the images themselves in their disposition across the picture plane. As I have said earlier, of all the elements that make up the graphic visual language, the quality of the outline is the most revealing, the most important, the most capable of bearing semantic and expressive meanings. *Cloudy* supports this view. King records the scene as if she is using a telescopic lens on the area the cat occupies and a wide-angled lens over the rest. Where Cloudy is, there is the focus. However small the image of the cat is, and however well she blends in with her surroundings (as indeed she claims to do in the text), she doesn't lose her identity.

The doublespread set in the garden, which reads, 'If the sun shines, I'll be stalking in the shadows' (page opening 4), displays King's technique perfectly. The left half depicts an expanse of sunlit lawn, which curves away between large shrubs. Long grasses and ox-eye daisies fringe the lower foreground. Substances are blurred and homogenized, painted in the loosest of forms: aqueous blobs of transparent tints of pink, blue and green and a pool of saturated acid yellow. The grasses nearest the beholder are as loosely defined as the far shrubs. The large-scale image of the cat occupies the right half of the picture as she pounces onto something hidden in the undergrowth beneath the trees on the far right. The two halves of the composition are united by a vertical passage where King introduces limited areas of detail in the shape of dapples of sunshine on shaded areas of the grass – the shade caused by overhanging trees which we cannot see but 'know' to be there because of the shade (an instance of King structuring the picture to promote the impression that we share Cloudy's three-dimensional space).

The focus is sharpening, and will continue to do so, as the beholder follows the action of the cat, which presents a strong falling diagonal emphasis. The viewpoint is level with the cat's, her body is in profile, and this area of the painting is in such sharp focus that the light catches individual hairs on her haunches. The grasses and bushes into which she leaps are also painted in detail; blades uncurl and spring up to reach the light, the branches display their ochre-red veined leaves, the colour of dried blood.

The experience of looking at the picture is very similar to

It the sun shines, I'll be stalking in the shadows.

the experience of looking at our visual field in real life. It is not so much that shapes on the periphery are blurred but that we are not giving our attention to what's over there. The tension King creates in this particular case means that we would like to be in two places at once, both of them pulsating with natural organic energy. The sun invites us to relish its dazzling intensity and warmth, but curiosity about the action of the cat is as great a draw. We too make the leap from impressions of light to mysterious depths (and with a picture book, being an extension of life, we are able to choose the moment in which to leap)

A sense of place

There is one point where King does not use this device of sharpening the focus on the cat irrespective of how near or far she is supposed to be in relation to the beholder (page opening 2). And that particular illustration emphasizes the sense of place, which is yet another dimension of the subjective experience of *Cloudy* as a whole. The text, which is sited on the lower right of the doublespread and in a very light tone, hints that 'When the rain pours you may catch sight of me in murky puddles'.

The painting shows a huge puddle spreading across the picture, with oblique bands of driving rain falling right to

45

left. The large inverted reflection of the cat moving from right to left in the top left of the picture is balanced by a band of tiny pebbles in the lower left foreground. The pebbles have slightly more saturated colour and are in sharper focus than anything in the rest of the composition. The passing of the cat's physical presence is recorded in a trail of paw marks on the path, pointing from right to left. The puddle itself is narrowest on the right and broadens across the picture plane towards the left in a series of curvilinear feline rhythms (another of those pictorial analogies). Even the tone of what is reflected in the puddle is darker towards the left.

The beholder's attention is being drawn from right to left, which has an interesting effect on the way we make sense of what is being shown. Perhaps because we read text from left to right, the sense of moving on through the sentences seems to be transferred to images. If they face right, we think of them as 'going'. In the painting the structure and visual dynamics lead me to believe that Cloudy is coming back from the expedition pictured on the preceding page opening.

We have noticed the sharpening of focus on Cloudy elsewhere in the book. What function does the device serve when applied to the pebbles? Quite simply, they draw attention to what is reflected in the puddle: not only the cat but also the cloudy skies and the trees in the spinney where she hunts.*

Further exemplification

Having considered how the abstract elements of the picture are able to inform the reading, let us consider how meaning is made from what is shown: cat, clouds and the trees. These are the major recurring images symbolizing the dominant themes of the picture book: independence, elusiveness, nature's cycles, and a range of associated meanings. That is to say, the cat, clouds and trees may be read as metaphorical images, which cannot look like what they represent because those qualities are abstract notions, but which may be displayed (in this case) through the series of pictures as a whole. Cat, trees and clouds act as expressive exemplifying symbols.

*If you enjoy interpictorial references or coincidences, look out for *Puddle* painted by M.C. Escher in 1952, which shows a similar play on water, reflections and footprints.

When the rain pours, you may catch sight of me in murky puddles.

Equally important, we understand the cat, trees and clouds as natural mimetic images, which look like what they represent or denote, but which also have literal meanings specific to this particular picture book. The trees act as topographic markers. When we notice these particular trees in this particular reflection, we actually know where we are standing as we look down into the puddle (we are on the prowl as well). As we recall seeing the trees in the previous composition, and recognize them in subsequent ones – pictured far away or nearby, stripped bare or in leaf, submitting to the gale or graven in cold moonlight – we take our bearings in Cloudy's territory which the trees literally exemplify.

Cloudy is remarkably free from anthropomorphic overtones. The cat is not a child in disguise. She's a prowler, a hunter, a killer with her eyes fixed on a dainty breakfast of chaffinch in the plum tree. In turn, a speeding car in the night might be the agent of her own death. The artist's skills give us an imaginative transformation which goes some way towards bridging the otherness between observer and what is being observed: not a real cat, of course, but Cloudy.

What I have been advocating through the close looking at *Cloudy* and *When Sheep Cannot Sleep* is active contemplation. I enjoyed both books at first glance, and then went on to try to find the source of my pleasure.

Cloudy
© 1989 Deborah King

47

Into the Classroom

I have formalized what I do in the classroom in a unit of work written in something like a diary form, recorded as the lessons progressed. This unit is tabulated on pages 70-71. I have also tied in the activity to the National Curriculum Programmes of Study for English, in relation to the Profile Components of Speaking and Listening, Reading, and Writing. I have suggested ways which would ensure continuity and progression across Key Stage 3. (In the tabulation the heading 'Language Development' serves to include cognitive and aesthetic development.)

I see the use of picture books as part of an education in developing a visual sense generally and in being able to make meaning from visual information in particular. Some of my reasons appear in the 'Justification' on pages 68-69.

I also believe that picture books can provide a valuable introduction to art appreciation – and why not? The ability to understand how meanings can be made from what is presented on the page will transfer and make easel paintings possibly more moving and certainly more interesting and accessible. The aesthetic activity required of the beholder when faced with line, shape and colour is much the same in both cases, although the form of the objects is different.

The total experience of a work of art includes the cultural assumptions we bring to it. Most people would find it easier to read a picture book than to respond to an easel painting. An informed beholder knows how much paintings and picture books have in common, not least in that both offer the opportunity for understanding and valuing art.

Another assumption is that the narratively oriented English picture-book tradition is the one by which all picture books should be judged. This is a limited view of what picture books are able to do, and so is the insistence that all we can do with them is tell stories. Who could complain if a raised awareness to colour via Kitamura or Wildsmith caused the violet-blue of a Piero della Francesca angel's robe to stop you in your tracks? Or do you take a metaphorical wander around in David Hockney's multi-perspective landscapes with any less pleasure because you can work out how cunningly he gives

48

you access, just like Sendak does in *Outside Over There*? Surely not.

The following unit of work is used with pupils of twelve to fourteen years, as the first stage of three units of work planned to raise visual awareness. In the term after the one in which pupils look at picture books, they read a novel and watch a film of it in order to study the different ways in which the same subject matter is treated: what has been gained, lost, changed, and the differences between being a reader and being a viewer. During the following term a study of advertising is made, and each pupil chooses examples and gives an oral presentation supported by visual aids (generally a short video clip of television advertising).

Unspoken Texts

A unit of work aimed at raising visual awareness,
using picture books as source material

Looking at pictures is a pleasurable activity, not regarded as 'work' by pupils, and pictures make satisfying subjects for investigation. Investigating something is also associated with pleasure: the excitement of discovering. Pupils bring with them more implicit knowledge than they know what to do with, and are ready for explicit knowledge in order to recognize the significance of what they already know, and to benefit from learning the (visual) language in which so much of today's communication is relayed.

Jerome Bruner maintained that any subject could be taught to any child in an intellectually honest form at any stage of her development; it was simply a matter of finding a 'courteous translation'. This I have attempted to do. Children like above all to get their hands upon the material and discover for themselves. What I had to do was give them the technical terms in which to describe what they found.

The lesson notes which follow have been used with pupils of a wide ability range in the age range of twelve to fourteen years. There is a substantial collection of picture books in the school library, but without any guidance top-ability children rarely seek them out. I have written the notes as a reflective record, hoping that the musings and asides are valuable. They

49

are supported by extracts from children's writing (pages 60-67) in order to give some indication of how the lessons were received. Finally, the notes are presented in a simple tabulation as a unit of work (pages 70-71).

The Lessons

(I have described the process in stages. How long each stage would take depends on the pupils' ability, interest, and concentration span. The total spans a period of four to six weeks.)

Materials: a box of picture books, greater in number than pupils in the group; some colour-sample sheets as supplied by art paint manufacturers, which give the names of the hues

Stage 1: Introduction

Ask class for examples of how they gain pleasure or information of all kinds from visual and audio-visual materials. List on chalkboard the range, from comics to the National Gallery, the news on television, advertisements on hoardings, films, videos, journals, etc.

Introduce the idea of interpreting what we see. If we have to be taught to read alphabetic signs, then might we not also have to be taught to read the visual sign language being employed in order to understand pictorial communications?

Tell students that we are going to look at picture books for a few weeks in order to discover, first, what pictures can do, and then how stories are made by the pictures, the words, and the book itself.

Throughout all, we will also keep in mind a couple of questions. What values are being promoted, and who is the reader to become – whose life are you sharing – during the reading?

But for the moment: 'Take a book, look and enjoy, make a note of anything of interest, should you so wish, then return the book to the box, take another book when you are ready.'
I ask them to do this in silence.

My observation: pupils look at the books for periods as short as three minutes. They are very silent – probably because being asked to look at picture books in classtime might seem rather odd, but also because by this stage of the lesson they have latched on to the idea that they are involved in something constructive and although not quite sure just what they might be looking for, they are indeed going to have a good look.

Stage 2: Thinking about the symbol system

I am immediately faced with the problem of asking the pupils to talk about pictures and write about pictures. But pictures (whether on the walls or on the page) are infinitely more than just 'painted words', to use Tom Wolfe's phrase, though we are going to have to reduce them to such.

I want to be sure to teach the students about respecting the differences between the two symbol systems – words and images. In picture books the burden of the storytelling rests on the art, but translating material from one symbol system into the other is reductionist. Talking about pictures is not the same as looking at them, and loss in translation must be acknowledged. This is a crucially important point.

Looking at pictures evokes emotional responses: the feeling, and a rationalization of how you feel. It is necessary to explain how feeling has a function: what makes your heart knock, what gladdens your eye sensuously, what affronts it – all this works upon your thinking processes.

Eye and mind together, as it were.

Begin lesson by talking about what the term 'symbol' means in this context. I write up the words 'music', 'pictures', 'sculpture', 'telling stories', 'reading stories', and ask the pupils to tell me how each one is communicated: what its language looks like, how its language appears.

We all reflect on the different ways in which each communicates. It's worth spending some time on this, drawing upon the shared implicit knowledge – students reflect readily on what they know, given encouragement. When the idea of different systems has been aired, we go back to looking at picture books.

My observation: a slightly more concentrated activity, as pupils look, and then exchange books.

Stage 3: Acquiring of a working vocabulary

Distribute picture books (some pupils now ask for particular texts) and loose-leaf paper, for note-making. Once pupils realize that musical notation and alphabet letters are sign languages for which we have names, they begin to understand that they will need a metalanguage in which to describe/refer to the visual signs of illustrative art.

But a picture book is an object as well as a collection of pictures and words, so we start with the object itself.

At all stages of the lesson, the gathering together of notes is done by posing a series of questions so that our technical vocabulary is arrived at through discussion, guesswork, deduction, drawing upon implicit knowledge via handling a picture book. Some of the terms will have to be taught through instruction. The questions begin with drawing attention to the physical features and working out why it is worth paying attention to them.

Cover
Picture-book stories very often begin on the cover. What are we to make of this? Just look at the very first picture you are being given, and file away that set of images for future reference. Who knows what you may be able to make from them later on.

Endpapers
Plain unworked colour, or patterned, or illustrated; here is more moodsetting, signalling and information. Note how the endpapers take you into the story. Who has a hardback edition, and who has a paperback edition? What is one of the differences between them?

Title page
Look at the typeface used, and the illustration – there is almost certain to be one – here is more evidence about how your reading is to be shaped.

Page opening
Since pictures often spread across two pages (a doublespread), or the text is set in opposition to the illustration, or the action from one page is continued on the next, giving us an uninterrupted view of future events, it is useful to use the term 'page opening' to describe the two

facing pages which present themselves as one unit.

Size

How does size affect your response to a book? Does the size encourage sharing or promote the idea of a one-to-one silent get-together? Is the size suggesting that this particular picture book is very special in some way because it is so very large or small?

Format

The picture book will be in a square, vertical or horizontal format. The format affects the shape which the artist fills with pictures. How does shape affect what an artist can show?

(Two pupils offer that a horizontal shape enables more space for backgrounds, settings. A lead is required to elicit that a vertical shape emphasizes characters who will appear on the page openings in comparatively large scale.)

A quick check here is done, by each pupil, looking at subject matter of picture book, and seeing if these theories hold. This leads to interesting discussion on how we use information gleaned from settings and appearances. Closer emphasis on a character in a vertical format might show us more about how that character feels. (Pupils with Charles Keeping's *The Highwayman, Beowulf,* and *The Wedding Ghost* wave about examples to make this point.)

Introduce concept of irony: as exhibited in life, literature, and in words and pictures interacting in picture books. In picture books, the pictures give you an idea of how the characters feel, and the pictures also indicate the emotional tone of the text. When the pictures appear to contradict the words, there is an acute irony at work.

A cursory glance at the illustrations won't tell you all you need to know.

Vocabulary continues with: layout, plate, frame, vignette, bleeds, border, montage. These terms refer to the ways in which an artist organizes visual material as shapes on a page opening. We discuss the effects of the different ways of presentation, using examples to hand.

Plenty of waving about of picture books, to show each other, to ask questions. The discussion demands a high level of reflection, and grasping for ways of describing.

53

More looking.

My observation: it is noticeable now that students are more directed in their looking, whispering to each other about the interesting features of individual picture books.

Stage 4: Visual investigations

I want to keep the technical aspect as simple as possible, and I remind myself that I cannot teach everything I know within a few lessons over a short period of time.

Each pupil chooses a picture book for personal study until the end of Stage 7 at least. Ask pupils to tell me what 'signs' lie on the picture plane. Very much teacher-led discussion arrived at:

- line (outline and textures and marks which indicate movement)
- colour
- objects represented in space.

What we see is made in a medium: ink, paint, crayon, pencil, charcoal, collage.

More looking ... finding words to describe what we see ... students brainstorm their observations onto the chalkboard. They make notes as and if they wish.

Line
Acts as a contour, or line representing a boundary between one thing and the next, in space. It may be used as shading to produce tone. Keeping supplies us with plenty of examples in *Beowulf*.

We find examples of bracelet shading where the lines follow form, and hatching and crosshatching. We discuss the effects.

Texture, which is often used to fill in a form, is perceived as a general quality of surface also made by line.

More looking, more deliberating.

I keep asking them if they see similarities between the picture book in hand and other illustrations, books at home, pictures they have seen elsewhere.

Students notice broken lines, used as convention, to suggest actions like shaking, or running.

Next we try to find words to describe the quality of the outline in the pictures before us. All offerings are listed on board, and examples include 'broken', 'continuous', 'fine', 'thick', 'scratchy'.

Several pupils now point out to me that quite often contours and colours overlap, or hit-and-miss. More discussion about effect. Try not to put words into their mouths.

Colour

Finding words to describe the over-all impression given by the colour scheme leads naturally into considering the medium and how it has been applied. Words like 'layered', 'transparent', 'blobby', 'thin' will emerge from pupils with encouragement.

I tell them about tone, referring simply to the lightness and darkness of colours. Plenty of time is needed at this stage because colour is often best described in apt similes and metaphors. 'Faded', 'moody', 'vibrant', 'bold' are the pupils' own ways of describing the effects of tone and saturation.

All the time I am encouraging them to reflect on how they feel about what they see.

Colour symbolism

This works in three main ways, as having:
  natural associations
  conventional associations
  associations particular to a specific book.

We think about the physical world, and colour in it. Discuss the effects of golden yellow, and red, from which we get natural associations such as happiness and warmth arising from our experience of sunshine and a welcome fire in winter.

We then think about our society and what colours signify by convention. Black, white, and green – sadness, evil: purity: political 'greens', associations with pixies/magic world – make the point.

And then, the value particular to a specific book is considered: one student offered us Sendak's *Dear Mili*, and said that a peachy-pink was symbolic of paradise and goodness, because of the way the artist had used that colour throughout the illustrations.

Another student noticed red in association with all kinds of dangers, in Anthony Browne's *Hansel and Gretel*, examples which embraced all three ways of colour symbolism. (This is a tremendous amount of information and might need to be spread over two lessons. It depends upon the interest and discussion generated.)

Stage 5: Visual investigations continued

Objects
Objects in space and viewpoint.

We first considered 'objects in space' in their abstract organization.

We reflected on the fact that the shapes of objects in themselves can suggest qualities such as delicacy, grace, awkwardness, energy. Examples were found of attenuated shapes and lines, and soft, full ones, and students tried to put the effect into words.

We looked at how the density of objects affects the mood of a picture, and how the sequence (which is the picture book) is affected. How we float along in uncluttered space in *Belinda's Balloon* and pick our way through the obstacle course of visual puns and jokes in *I Hate My Teddy Bear*.

A different frame of mind is required for each reading.

Then there are the internal tensions and psychological effects caused by where the objects are sited: how we 'read' rising and falling diagonal emphases, the weight that is given to an object in the lower as opposed to the upper half of the picture plane, how a triangle suggests stability, but how an inverted triangle implies a fast fall.

(Remember the figure of the highwayman in Keeping's illustrations for the Noyes poem, when the eponymous hero is shot 'down like a dog on the highway' and sprawls, head first and limbs spread, visually assaulting the beholder?)

Objects as 'carriers of meaning'.

An object represents itself (a mimetic form), but also it will

56

represent more than itself. It carries cultural meanings, it will carry meanings specific to that particular book, and the viewer will bring personal associations to that object.

We look at the dandelion which the little boy gives to the UFO in Kitamura's *UFO Diary* . The dandelion is a worthless weed, but pretty enough for the child to like it; symbolically it represents a living gift for another planet; it exemplifies friendship, generosity and trust, and so on.

And if the object is in colour and tone, these will create further conventional, cultural and specific associations, further opportunities for exemplification.

I do not attempt to introduce systems of perspective but we talk about viewpoint – the bird's eye, eye-to-eye, worm's-eye views – and study the effects. We also consider whether we are being shown the pictured world in close-up (large scale), middle distance, or long shot (small scale). Children have implicit knowledge about involving and distancing techniques, from their experience of television drama and film. All they need is help to reflect on the significance of what they know.

Again, this is a tremendous amount of information and might need to be spread, or diluted. It depends upon the interest and discussion generated, and to some extent upon the ability of the group.

Stage 6: Putting words to the pictures

Again I have to remind myself that everything that might be said cannot be covered in this particular unit of work.

To begin with, the students and I consider how the words of the text tell us what to look at and what we might look out for: words guide us, as we scan the whole picture. Research shows that the reader scans the picture first, then reads the text, then returns to the picture to reinterpret in the light of the words. The words help us to interpret the pictures and vice versa.

But be careful. The words might not always mean what they say. If the words say one thing and the pictures show something rather different, we have a relationship based upon irony.

57

Good examples of this arise in McAfee and Browne's *The Visitors Who Came to Stay* and Paul and Carter's *Captain Teachum's Buried Treasure*. The irony of the title page of *When the Wind Blows*, where Jim reads *The Times* for information beneath a sign which says 'Silence', is not overlooked by a pupil who has that book to hand.

Even if the words and the pictures support each other without apparent contradiction, the pictures will convey an emotional mood; they will show something which the brief, declarative text does not say. They will exemplify feelings and states of being.

It is this faculty of exemplification that is a central feature of the aesthetic experience.

There is good opportunity here for reflection upon how literary prose and poetry and fine arts exemplify.

Stage 7: Reading a picture book

By now we recognize that reading words and looking at pictures are very complex activities. We need to be aware of and accommodate how the speeds of reading the text and 'reading' the pictures differ. With the text, we want to read on, to find out what is going to happen – we are driven by the narrative thrust. But the pictures require us to stay, look, search, reflect – they interrupt the text at regular intervals, and sometimes, as in *Where the Wild Things Are*, the text disappears as the illustrations take over.

I think we have recognized that, while we might get the story told by the text in a matter of minutes, there are as many more stories waiting to be made as times we are prepared to re-search the illustrations. What each of us does in effect is to read the two texts, put them together, and create a composite text – one that exists in the maker's head only.

I explain that no two readers will make a composite text which is identical. That's exciting. And creative.

Back to looking.

Stage 8: Writing about a picture book

There is a chance here to keep or to change the picture book the pupil has been studying. What matters most is that the pupil likes whatever is the focus of the written piece. Welcome pupils' picture books brought in from home, if they wish to study them.

The task is to write about a picture book with an awareness of its form, in any way which the pupil chooses. I suggest a method for gathering notes:

- skim the lot to get the flavour
- then read the text carefully on its own
- then 'read' the pictures, noting anything which claims attention in any way:
  - dominant colour
  - tone
  - scale
  - repetition of shapes, objects, layout (much as one would read a poem, noting the figures of speech, rhythms, rhyme, punctuation, verse form).
- Then keep asking, 'what is the effect of what I am noticing?' in the sequence of illustrations
- think about the work as a whole
- then put the words to pictures and ask about the nature of the relationship between what is being said and what is being shown
- and keep looking because there is always more discovering to be done.

Note: presented as a series of lessons, my notes suggest a teacher-dominated activity, but all the students contributed all the time, once initial guidance had been given about a particular feature. The writing task was undertaken independently, two weeks of class time (in this case, eight classes of fifty minutes each, and homework) being allowed for the process. The weekly library lesson was given over to looking at illustrated books of all kinds, especially those concerned with Fine Art.

Follow-up work

Examples of pupils' written work are given below. The pupils' reviews were varied in form, and various too were the emphases, as may be seen in the briefer extracts which follow the one review which is reproduced in full.

'A Dream of a Picture Book'
A review of *Can it be true?* by Susan Hill
illustrated by Angela Barrett
published by Hamish Hamilton, 1988

This story by Susan Hill is a beautiful prose poem. It is a variation of a traditional nativity theme, seen from a different point of view from most nativity tales. *Can it be true?* tells the story of people from all over the world, dreaming on Christmas Eve. The people dream they are going to the stable, and the book portrays this by showing animals and people from all walks of life travelling to find the saviour. It is a very serene and gentle book, perfect for a Christmas story.

The text is highly poetic, and seems dreamy and mystical. But when placed next to the beautiful illustrations and borders, it fades because the reader's attention is caught by the pictures. Without the pictures, the text would be less dramatic. The pictures seem to make sense of the text.

The story portrays the whole world as one small crowd of people. It does not really have any main characters, with the exception of Jesus at the end. Jesus is the only person in the whole book who is portrayed as a recognisable character. All the other animals and people in the book are part of the group going to find the saviour.

The group represents society. It is thought provoking that all the humans in the book seem to be fighting and killing. The general dreams of war, while the toys on the nursery floor are soldiers. The general dreams of war, and the children play of war. From childhood to death, humans are obsessed with greed and war. Maybe this is the author's idea of how humans are.

But once the Christ figure is born, society changes and people become nicer to each other. All the animals hear 'the message'. They stop fighting and killing, and travel together to find Jesus. The whale pulls the whaler's boat, the mouse rides on the cat's back, and the shrew has a ride on the owl.

When they arrive at the stable, the animals all kneel together and gaze with wonder at their saviour. This is the climax of the dream.

Images

The book is beautifully illustrated by Angela Barrett. The images are etched in ink. Due to the ink, the line in the book is very grainy and broken. She uses hatching and cross-hatching to show depth in her pictures. This also gives the effect of gloom and darkness.

The images are painted in a style which makes the book very natural and serene. The book is full of muted colours, predominantly blues and greens. The pictures depict ordinary everyday objects, which reinforces this impression.

The final picture is a lot brighter and more colourful than the others. Until the last picture all the illustrations have been cold blues and greys, with occasional splashes of colour (such as the fox or stained glass window). The final picture is mostly composed of reds and oranges which radiate from Jesus.

Although the pictures seem simple, they are really quite complex. Each page contains a hidden theme. One doublespread shows many ways of telling time, from standing stones to a dandelion and the moon.

The borders on this page contain things that relate to the main picture. The staff and fencing link with the sheep, the eggs relate to the hens, and the worm is surrounded by a border containing spiders and centipedes.

The pictures relate to the text. The text says: 'It was Christmas Eve, on the farm, in the fields, in the streets of the town.' The pictures portray this with images of a farm, fields and streets in a town. This would make the text very easy for a young child to understand.

This could of course be portrayed in the opposite way – the text relates to the pictures which identify with the borders.

The images have very bright borders which are brighter than the pictures themselves. Often part of the picture extends over the frame, giving the impression that the frames can be broken. While the illustrator uses the border to set the confines of the picture, she breaks her own rule and teases the reader by letting the picture break loose from the frame.

This bordering applies all the way through the book except for the last page when they get to the crib. Here the border is greatly reduced, allowing the reader to concentrate on the picture of the crib scene.

Christmas Eve and twelve
chimed the clock
on the church
in the town
on the wall
in the hall,
when the message was heard.

Christmas Eve.

Themes

There are several themes in the book, including dreams and the passage of time.

The theme of time suggests the journey of life and that your time is running out – because you don't know when you are going to die. It also relates to the title of the book *Can it be true?* It asks whether the time has really come yet for Christ to be born.

On the front cover Angela Barrett has painted a clock tower, the time showing 20 to 12. As the book progresses, it gets nearer to twelve until the clocks chime and the saviour is born.

The Trinity is a recurrent theme, symbolising God the father, God the son, and God the Holy Ghost. It appears as three angels, three men, and three stars.

Other numbers also appear. Twelve people surround the baby, and thirteen stars shine in the sky (the thirteenth being Jesus). The other three people around the crib are Mary, Joseph and Mary Magdalene.

Another recurrent theme is that of opposites, symbolising war. Each character is paired with its opposite: the cat threatens the mouse, the whaler hunts the whale, and the wolf eyes the sheep. The animals in the book are split into

Two doublespreads from
Can it be true?
words by Susan Hill
illustrations copyright
© *1988 Angela Barrett*

two groups, either hunting like the owl or cat or being hunted like the shrew.

The book is written as if in a dream: maybe the whole book is a dream. The front endpapers show pictures of children dreaming, while the back endpaper shows a child looking at a Christmas tree. Maybe the child has woken up: the dream is over and it is Christmas day, and the dream has come true.

In Thomas Hardy's poem 'The Oxen', he sums up the feel of the whole book – how wonderful it would be to see Jesus in the crib at Christmas. If someone asked the poet to go with him, he would believe them and not even be surprised if he saw the oxen kneeling. This poem has partly inspired the book – it says how wonderful it would be if everyone dropped their hatred and just for Christmas went to see Jesus, and got on together.

To summarise this review, the title *Can it be true?* means, 'Is the message true?' Having re-read the book, the title also means 'Is there a God?' or 'Has the Saviour come?' *Can it be true?* is the story of the First Christmas, which means different things to different parts of society.

*

The longest review ran to twenty-six typed pages which discussed the themes, ideology, imagery, and language of *When the Wind Blows*. The pupil is able to sustain a two-page discussion of two page openings depicting the explosion of the atomic bomb, only a flavour of which we may catch here. She begins with a doublespread and moves on to the two single plates: how she 'senses' that it is a very powerful picture and

I can sense too, the mass devastation that is occurring within it ... Raymond Briggs has done a terrific job capturing the effect of a nuclear bomb so well on paper. The red/pink symbolises the immense heat and the white symbolises the light and raw power.

She notes later that

having the colours so bright and explosive helps me to understand the power the bomb contains, and the seriousness and importance of this picture compared with the others. The other clue is that, not only are these pictures so different in comparison with any previous ones, they are also at about the centre of the book. I draw the conclusion that these pictures are the most important in the book and that everything else seems to revolve around them.

Another student conducted a little ethnographical research on *UFO Diary*. Having commented on the visual features, using metalanguage accurately, she then reports how she gave an adult and a child of six, first the text minus title and pictures, and then the complete picture book. She recorded their comments and asked for their 'reviews'. She discovered (of course) that the pictures affect very much what you understand the story to mean. She writes that the child reviewer made the natural mistake of assuming that the boy comes out of the UFO when it first arrives, because he is featured with a ladder which he could have come down. Coming down or going up? This puzzle is a very neat demonstration of how a very young reader is not always as skilled at deduction as the artist assumes.

Interpreting *Dear Mili* might well give anyone a puzzling experience. In Grimm's tale a child is sent by her mother into a forest to escape the dangers of war. She finds sanctuary in

the house of St Joseph, and discovers a friend much like
herself to play with. On the third day she returns home to
discover that she has been in the forest thirty years, for her
mother is now an old woman. Reunited, they die. As this
pupil writes, 'the pictures tell the same story but in different
form'.

A woman lives with her daughter. Danger comes, because
flames are drawn roaring fiercely out of the clouds and the
mother takes the child into the forest.

Everything then becomes livid and cinnamon-coloured
except what is mentioned in the text, which stands out
more. Then the child sits to rest in the forest surrounded
by trees. Yet the trees are rather extraordinary and are
drawn like humans, each tree is skinny and looks as if it's
dead which implies the child is gradually coming to her
death. In the first pictures there is a guardian angel
watching over the child but in this picture the angel is
asleep which means that guardian angels are hopeless
because he wasn't preventing her from death. The girl is
not the only one dying because other children seem to be
walking over a bridge, dressed very dimly. The structure of
the bridge is made of seven crosses and there are also seven
children on the bridge so the bridge symbolises the death
of the children. She then comes to a rose tree with
extravagant roses with each petal flowering but if the
previous picture symbolises mortality then the harmony of
the rose tree symbolises a new life in a wonderland which
to us is known as heaven.

Two pages later comes the most caring picture of all. It is
affectionate and tranquil. The child is serving St Joseph
who is a godly figure with long white flowing hair. The
child looks dainty and courteous in this picture and St
Joseph talks to her. The feet of the characters look
tremendously big which I understand looks as if there are
adventures ahead.

The girl wakes in the morning. Sunflowers surround the
small bedroom. They symbolise happiness. She goes into
the wonderland, and meets a child who is also pretty, like
an angel without wings. Then there is a doublespread. This
is when the children from the bridge re-appear. Their facial
expressions look content and each one sings merrily. There
are roses and orchids growing around the page, each one
vermilion and orange. There are tombstones hidden among

the luscious grass, which I assume belong to the children. St Joseph tells Mili that the time has come for her to return home and hands her a blooming rose. She says goodbye to her companion and heads back home. She arrives home to discover her mother very old, which implies that the girl's been reincarnated. The last doublespread shows her mother reaching out her arms to clasp her child and there are many crosses and a tombstone slightly poking out of the ground. All these symbolise death. So it was as if the child came back to take her mother to the place known to us as heaven.

This young reader-viewer has made her own sense of Sendak's interpretation.

Another pupil has little trouble with character analysis in *The Wedding Ghost*. She writes:

One of the pictures shows people on a train reading with interest about things which are of complete contrast to their looks. My favourite example is a grotesque, wrinkled old lady who is reading *Cosmopolitan* which has a pretty, skinny model in a very skimpy bikini, posing on the cover! I think that it is showing what deep down inside these people want to be like.

Quasimodo Mouse is called 'a travelling book':

The action is always moving from left to right pushing you on and on until finally when Quasimodo and his mate reach the seaside the cliffs form a barrier, stopping you and slowing the story down in just the right place. Three-quarter plates are nearly always used, with the text to one side or another. Occasional double spreads are used to increase the impact of the picture. On one double spread the artist uses four small pictures to speed up the action even more, to get you to the seaside.

No difficulties here in recognizing the part played by the layout. This student writes well about the style, effects of paint-spattering techniques, variations in colour density, volume, and bold and broken lines. I asked him if he had surprised himself with his writing. He retorted that he had surprised his father most.

And the final example, taken from a review of *Strat and Chatto*, shows a pupil struggling to turn impression into

'Do you live in the belfry?' Chatto said.

'No,' Strat said, 'I have a pad in that place over there.'

'The place where it says CONDEMNED on the door?' Chatto said. 'That's a funny name for a house.'

'It means 'Beautiful View' in Latin,' Strat said.

'Now, about these mice.'

'One mouse,' said Chatto. 'I've eaten the others but this one eludes me. It sits on the fridge and drops lentils on my head.'

'Let's have a dekko,' said Strat, and he climbed through the cat flap.

information and to relate the style to another pictorial genre.

The out lines of this picture book is very thin whiskery lines. Most of the animals are insects are drawn with lots of lots of lines. But some parts are painted very pale colours. I think the artist thinks the faces are more imporant than the bodys because the faces are more ecspersion. the cartoon style, not like in Walt Disney but like you see in newspapers of politicians. The animals human expresions.

Acknowledgement: With thanks to Charlotte, Sian, Melissa, Catherine, Helen, Thomas and Scott.

Strat and Chatto
words by Jan Mark
illustration copyright
© *1989 David Hughes*

THE PICTURE BOOK

Unspoken Texts, within the National Curriculum in English

This unit will explore the interaction of

Audience - Text-type - Purpose

through Speaking and Listening, Reading, and Written Response

This unit looks at   Communication
                     Ways of telling
                     Response
                     Nature of reading - developing
                     Strategies

Elements: Media - Story - Genre

Justification

-    teach children explicitly that, just as they have learnt to
read the written word beyond its surface signs, so they need to
learn how visual language works. The acquisition of such knowledge
may be justified, since we live in an audio-visual age of
communication.

Media

-    enable the child/emergent adult to be much more aware of
the moral and didactic functions of art and images, issues of
politics and ideology encountered on screen, billboards, in
magazines, newspaper, and within the covers of graphic novels.

Story

-    dispel the popular misunderstanding that looking at pictures
is largely a matter of seeing what they denote, i.e. what
stories may be made through the recognition of objects as their
mimetic (literal) selves. Picture books for older children,
as well as signifying denotatively, will signify through
exemplification: i.e. they are expressive works of art,
exemplifying states of being, moral values, moods, etc.
Children need to be taught about the object-as-symbol, and
encouraged to think about relationships - webs of association,
meanings which objects are able to signify.

Genre

-    teach children about creative strategies: those needed to
understand the picture-book form, and those employed by the
makers of picture books.

Programmes of Study

Media   AT2 - "Reading should include picture books..." (3)
               - "talk about the ways in which language is
                  written down..." (6)
               - "appreciate the significance of print and the
                  fact that pictures and other visual media can
                  also convey meaning..." (7)

		-	"Pupils should be taught to interpret and use ... changes of print or typeface..." (13)
		-	"Pupils should be taught to handle, and be given experience in using, a range of information texts in a variety of media." (17)
		-	"Pupils should be introduced to a range of media texts, and be encouraged to consider their purpose, effect and intended audience." (18)

Story   AT2   - "be shown how to read different kinds of materials in different ways." (10)

Genre   AT1   - "listen and respond to an increasing range of fiction..." (6)
- "engage in prediction, speculation and hypothesis in the course of group activity..." (6)
- activities should include "talking about stories... and other texts" (8)
- pupils should be encouraged to "express their opinions and to argue a point of view, to be receptive to the contributions of others and make their own contributions effectively..." (13)

       AT2   - "Reading should include picture books..." (3)
- "Schools must provide as wide a range [of works] as possible." (9)
- "Teachers should discuss texts which make imaginative use of English." (13)
- Pupils should read "a variety of genres". (14)

The Written Outcome   - AT 3,4,5

- "Pupils should be helped to recognise explicitly the different stages of the writing process." (23)
- "write in a range of forms, including book reviews..." (25)
- "Record their first thoughts, capture immediate responses and collect and organise ideas so that they are available for reflection." (25)
- "write for a range of purposes including.. book reviews..." (25)
  "write for a range of purposes including... expressing a point of view." (25)
- "Pupils should come to understand the functions of the impersonal style..." (28)
- "Pupils should develop a sensitivity to the different styles of vocabulary that are used in different types of writing." (29)

Suggestions for Further Work with Picture Books

Study of group/collection of picture books linked by content or theme and explored for values: to include fairy and folk tales from a variety of cultures.

Making a picture book: broad study of characteristics gained from a box of picture books. Pupil to make a picture book for a specified audience or recipient.

Unspoken Texts: an introduction to visual imagery in pictures and a study of the picture-book form.
The model for this tabulation was developed by the National Association for the Teaching of English.

EXPERIENCE AND ACTIVITIES	LANGUAGE DEVELOPMENT	TEACHER INTERVENTION
		Organizes a box of picture books, sufficient in number for at least one per pupil
Private reading - viewing.		Introduces topic - states aims. Points out unique nature of picture-book form. Distributes books. Invites pupils to read, exchange, change picture books. Asks for silent reading. Observes behaviour, especially speed with which pupils renew picture books.
Consideration of concept of symbol systems. Private reading - viewing.	Reflecting on different ways the systems communicate, and difficulties of translating from one system to another without loss of meaning.	Symbol systems: talks about music, visual art, spoken and written languages. Talks about the function of feeling in the cognitive (reasoning) process. Distributes picture books, as before.
Consider the picture book as a physical object. Make careful notes. Class discussion of examples from individual picture books.	Acquisition of a working vocabulary. Gathering of notes is done by posing a series of questions so that many answers arrive through class discussion. Some technical terms learned through instructions. Metalanguage in use, as pupils discuss effects of different ways of presentation. Pupils "show" examples from picture books, ask questions, make points. The discussion demands a high level of reflection, and grasping for ways of describing.	Draws attention to: Cover, endpaper, title page, page opening, size, typeface, format. Vocabulary continues with: layout, plate, frame, vignette, bleed, border, montage. Teacher chairs discussion. Encourages quiet pupils to contribute.
Each pupil selects one book for close study. Visual investigations of "signs". Note-making continues.	Acquisition of metalanguage continues, via teacher-led discussion: whole class. Pupils "show" examples, as before.	Teacher leads discussion, and defines: medium, line, colour symbolism. Invites pupils to supply examples.

EXPERIENCE AND ACTIVITIES	LANGUAGE DEVELOPMENT	TEACHER INTERVENTION
Listening, note-making, searching the picture book.	Language development continues, through observation and reflection and discussion. Pupils draw upon implicit knowledge.	Teaches about pictured objects as themselves, and as carriers of meanings which are cultural, personal, and unique to this particular picture book.
Pupils keep the selected picture book. Focus upon story told by words. Look at pictures separately, then read words and pictures "as a whole". Individual activity. Note-making as necessary.	Pupils understand that the words help to interpret the picture and vice versa.	Asks pupils to consider relationship of words and illustrations.
Pupils spend entire period with chosen picture book.	Reflect on all the knowledge gained.	Explains concept of exemplification in literature and the arts, and how works of art are able to be expressive.
Pupils work with chosen book, considering the processes involved in reading the book as a whole.	Pupils aware of processes of reading two texts, and making a third one "in the head". Understand how rhythms of reading a picture book have to be accommodated. While there is a desire to "read-on" set up by the verbal text, the pictures require us to stay, look, search, reflect.	Emphasizes the individual, creative nature of making composite text. Tells pupils that the 'Written Outcome' is the next step. Pupils may wish to bring in their own picture books from home, especially if ethnic minority.
Preparation for 'Written Outcome'. Pupils keep selected book or make another choice. Decide on the form the review will take.	Pupils gather notes by: looking at picture books as object, skim read, read text carefully, read pictures carefully, noting anything which claims attention in any way (dominant colour, tone, scale, repetition of shapes, objects). Ask themselves what is the effect of what is being noticed, put words to pictures, make composite text, draft, edit, publish.	Acts as adviser for children who want to use the same picture books. Helps everyone to find a picture book which appeals. Sets task: write about a picture book with an awareness of its form, in any way the pupils choose. Allows two weeks for writing process, circulates, observes, encourages, edits.

On the Bookshelf

Once we start thinking about picture books as aesthetic objects, which is not the same as thinking about them as tools for literacy and language development, we discover that we do not understand them at all well, however familiar they may be to us. Not much has been written about the picture-book form itself, or about the aesthetic experience it offers, but at least our understanding of pictures can be helped by accounts of the cognitive development of aesthetic experience in relation to art, theories about the psychology of perception, of symbol systems. Not only do we find out about the various 'ways of seeing', we also come to appreciate the significance of what we already know.

Rather than supply a 'recommended reading list' of daunting length, what follows is a set of notes about a very few books, each one of which has helped me. These are the books to which I return again and again and which are read alongside works of literary theory, in my repeated attempts to understand various aspects of the picture book. These are the authors whose work (and words) inform my own writing.

Howard Gardner
Artful Scribbles:
The Significance of
Children's Drawings
Basic Books, 1980

Rhoda Kellogg
Analysing Children's Art
National Press Books
1969/70

Michael J. Parsons
How We Understand Art
Cambridge Univ. Press
1987

Since picture books are primarily intended for children, we could well begin by trying to understand their viewpoint. The psychologist Howard Gardner has written at length about children's conception of the arts and their sensitivity to painting styles, while the work of Rhoda Kellogg tells us about illustration by children. A particularly interesting and relevant book, since we introduce and share picture books with children, is Michael J. Parsons' *How We Understand Art: A Cognitive Developmental Account of Aesthetic Experience*. Parsons studies how we come to make sense of art, and he argues that works of art are, first of all, aesthetic objects, and their significance is lost when they are regarded as if they are just ordinary objects. His book reflects mainstream views, and the philosophers whom he acknowledges as having influenced him are Collingwood, Langer, Dewey, and Danto.

Parsons' views are, firstly, that 'art is not just a series of pretty objects; it is a way of articulating our interior life'. His second belief is that 'what art expresses is more than what one person has in mind at one time' and that 'an understanding of expression in the arts, when it is at all complicated, is a social and historical construction'. The third theme is that 'judgements about art are capable of being objective'.

Using paintings as his focus, and findings from a decade of fieldwork with viewers from kindergarten pupils to university students and their mentors, Parsons hypothesizes that our understanding of art develops in a particular way: that we reach the complex understanding of our maturity through five stages that cover a span of time and follow each other sequentially. Our progress is built upon a series of insights into the possibilities of art. Where we end up in this sequence depends on what kinds of art we encounter and how far we have been encouraged to think about them; it is not an organic process and the stages are not related to age except in the very early years.

Parsons' account of staged development suggests an all too orderly progress, and there are many reasons for questioning his hypothesis (including the doubt that it could hold up cross-culturally). However, I value his book because much of the account is familiar. I experience – in a more fragmented version – the stages he defines, and I also recognize the verbal responses which he has recorded and which I hear all the time from the children and students with whom I share picture books. Parsons' strength is that he invites us to be reflective about the assumptions we make, what insights we already have, and he may well give us many more.

Art and Visual Perception: A Psychology of the Creative Eye – The New Version by Rudolf Arnheim offers theories about why we see what we do, and why we feel as we do, when we look at pictures. What enables us to know that Ida's world is going out of kilter when the goblins steal her baby sister in *Outside Over There,* or that Toby's head is metaphorically 'in a spin' in *Through the Magic Mirror*? Why is Carroll's portrayal of Alice suggestive of extreme vulnerability, while Tenniel's Alice is altogether a much more robust creature and sensuous image, and how does Zwerger's raw-skinned Little Red-Cap command our sympathy while countless other images of that character leave us unmoved?

You might well find answers to satisfy you in Arnheim's work. He believes that a work of art presents a carefully contrived experience for an observer, and his intention is to

Rudolf Arnheim
Art and Visual Perception
Univ. California Press
1974

show us just how 'the perceived image, not the paint, is the work of art'. He organizes his survey of the structural elements of art into ten chapters – Balance, Shape, Form, Growth, Space, Light, Colour, Movement, Dynamics, and Expression – and is at pains to stress that these are not to be regarded as a checklist to be placed alongside a work of art. Vision is not a mechanical recording of these elements, but the apprehension of significant structural patterns. There is no point in hunting for visual shapes unless it is to see what they may tell us. He shows the structural elements at work through numerous illustrations – diagrams, line drawings, half-tones, colour plates – thus helping us to 'see' more clearly.

The principles of his psychological thinking derive from gestalt theory, and the experiments he cites are designed to show that the appearance of any element depends on its place and function in an over-all pattern. If we wish to be 'admitted to the presence of a work of art', as he puts it,

> we must, first of all, face it as a whole. Safely guarded by the structure of the whole, we then try to recognize the principal features and explore their dominion over dependent details. Gradually, the entire wealth of the work reveals itself and falls into place, and as we perceive it correctly, it begins to engage all the powers of the mind with its message.

Arnheim is not concerned much with the extent to which learned responses feature in visual perception, so the work of Ernst Gombrich provides a counterbalance.

E.H. Gombrich
Art and Illusion
Phaidon Press 1977

In his great classic, *Art and Illusion, A study in the psychology of pictorial representation*, Ernst Gombrich presents his theories on the psychological aspect of image making and image reading, and on the relative share of nature and convention in imagery itself. His book is structured broadly into three sections: first, he discusses the artist's contribution, next the beholder's share, then a synthesis which overtly draws the matter of representation to the realm of aesthetics and moral values. It is an accessible study of perception and optical illusion, and all that is required of its reader is a comfortable chair, curiosity, and plenty of patience. Gombrich takes nine chapters to arrive at what he calls the

74

'emotional core' of art, but since the reading matter is amply illustrated, and his concepts challenging, our 'approach through the quicksands of perceptual theory' is never plodding.

His study is particularly interesting for the student of picture books since he is concerned with the riddle of style – why it is that different ages and different nations have represented the visible world in such different ways. In following Gombrich's arguments, we beholders are given leads into how to look at the diverse styles of illustrators and ask questions about the illusion involved in their art, and what collaborative acts are required in order to transform a series of pieces of paper into a world in which we believe. According to Gombrich, every artist is shaped by the tradition from which he emerges; his 'seeing' is conditioned by the habits and conventions of his culture. The application of such a theory to picture-book artists is fruitful.

Consider the work of Maurice Sendak. Ask who his predecessors were, what traditional schematic conventions of image-making he inherited from them and used when he was making the illustrations for the Grimm Brothers collection, or for *Outside Over There*, or *Dear Mili*, or for the early work, *Moon Jumpers*, and you will discover that Sendak works strongly within the Northern Romantic tradition. But according to Gombrich, under the pressure of exceptional demands a great artist is able to break out of 'the prison of style' that he has inherited. Sendak is one such – with his picture book *Where the Wild Things Are*, which extended the boundaries of the form – and succeeding artists benefit from his experience.

Applying Gombrich's theory to artists whose work is not directly within the English narratively oriented picture-book tradition helps us to appreciate difference in style. For example, Satoshi Kitamura is a Japanese artist living in London, and the background of many of his picture-book illustrations is the streets of the capital. Nevertheless, when he structures a composition, he frequently applies the conventions of the Far East. This is why his pictorial style seems so fresh to Western eyes.

There is so much to be learnt from Gombrich. It will have to suffice here to say that if you are curious about the appeal of texture in illustrations – why Jane Hissey's style and Robert

Ingpen's style have your fingers tingling to reach out and touch – then Gombrich can tell you about the appeal of light over form. If you want purchase on the puzzle about why a particular pose or arrangement of forms has the power to touch your emotions, then begin by considering that great art has less to do with pictorial fidelity and more to do with an artist finding 'equivalences' for experiences.

Richard Wollheim
Painting as an Art
Thames & Hudson 1987

The guiding theme of Richard Wollheim's *Painting as an Art* is the nature of pictorial meaning in painting. Wollheim's general account of pictorial meaning locates the latter in a triad of factors:

> the mental state of the artist, the way this causes him to paint, and the experience that a suitably informed and sensitive spectator can be expected to have on looking at the artist's picture.

Wollheim calls this 'a psychological account', and it sets him against philosophers who propose to explain pictorial meaning by transposing it into linguistic meaning – schools of thought which include structuralism and semiotics.

Wollheim posits a duality of roles for the spectator, who is both outside the picture and located within the virtual space that the painting represents. The inner spectator has a special relationship with the expressive content of the picture. The artist relies upon the spectator to have and to use three fundamental perceptive capacities: 'seeing-in', expressive perception, and the ability to experience visual delight. Upon these perceptual capacities rest the three basic powers that belong to painting: the power to represent external objects, the power to express mental or internal phenomena, and the power to induce a special form of pleasure.

Wollheim demonstrates his own remarkable capacities through a series of lucid interpretations of the work of old and modern masters. For those of us predominantly interested in picture-book art, what he has to say on the processes we go through as spectators gives insights into a number of difficult issues.

The word 'aesthetic' is used very loosely by the layperson, and academic disciplines give it different meanings. If you use the term but would find it difficult to explain what you mean by it, then try reading some of the works of Nelson Goodman (a radically different approach from Wollheim's), and see if he helps you with your thinking. He will tell you exactly what processes he believes you should be experiencing in front of a picture and, after all your hard work, will offer an explanation as to why it is impossible to be verbally precise about what a picture means.

Nelson Goodman's *Languages of Art* and *Of Mind and Other Matters* contain material which is relevant to how we use picture books because we are bringing two symbol systems together (words and images) as we make our way from cover to cover.

Nelson Goodman
Languages of Art
Hackett 1976

Of Mind
and Other Matters
Harvard Univ. Press 1984

In *Languages of Art* Goodman constructs a general theory of symbols: an important study of the conventions operating in different symbolic forms such as scores, dance, dramatic scripts, texts, paintings, diagrams, maps, and models.

In his theory of aesthetic meaning, Goodman distinguishes the two ways in which visual symbols in paintings refer: denotation and exemplification – terms which are convenient to use when we try to consider the different meanings that can be attached to a single image. Goodman alerts us to how much awaits our attention as we scan an illustration, the richness of reference, and the impossibility of translating into words exactly what we see. Nevertheless, he would not have us deterred from trying.

Goodman has no patience with the notion that the aesthetic attitude in front of a picture is 'passive contemplation of the immediately given' any more than that the appropriate aesthetic attitude towards a poem amounts to gazing at the printed page without reading it. He believes that we have to read the former as well as the latter. He describes the aesthetic attitude as dynamic, 'restless, searching, testing – less attitude than action: creation and re-creation'.

Goodman recognizes that we do not part easily with the idea that art is in some way more emotive than science or that the aesthetic experience is somehow emotive rather than cognitive. We also tacitly accept what he calls a 'domineering dichotomy', which causes us to place sensation, perception, inference, conjecture, investigation, fact and truth on one side and pleasure, pain, interest, satisfaction, all branches of spontaneous affective response on the other. This keeps us from seeing that in aesthetic experience the emotions function cognitively.

> The work of art is apprehended through the feeling as well as the senses ... Emotion in aesthetic experience is a means of discerning what properties a work has and possesses.

In *Of Mind and Other Matters* Goodman returns to some of the material in *Languages of Art*, clarifies points, refutes arguments which have been forwarded by fellow philosophers and critics, and explores new subjects. He also refers back to his work, *Ways of Worldmaking*. Of particular interest is what he writes about the relationship between words and thoughts, what we think *in* and what we think *of*, which is pertinent to understanding better what it is to read a picture book. Goodman is not concerned with a way of teaching art appreciation so much as with furthering alert and intelligent looking.

W. J. T. Mitchell
Iconology: Image, Text
Ideology
Univ. Chicago Press 1986

Because I consider picture books to be cultural objects I return again and again to *Iconology: Image, Text, Ideology* by W.J.T. Mitchell, which is a study of the 'logos' (words, ideas, discourse, or 'science') of 'icons' (images, pictures, likenesses). This collection of essays is concerned with the description and interpretation of visual art, and the ways in which images seem to speak for themselves by persuading, telling stories, or describing. After discussing the idea of imagery, Mitchell goes on to give us a series of close readings of a few important texts in the theory of imagery.

The readings revolve around two historical centres, one in the late eighteenth century, the other in the era of modern criticism. The texts are by Nelson Goodman, Ernst Gombrich, G.E. Lessing and Edmund Burke.

Obviously, in order to appreciate Mitchell's book fully, and to follow his analysis into the third and final part, 'Images and Ideology', in which he discusses 'the image as the site of a special power that must either be contained or exploited', his reader needs to be familiar with all the key texts he discusses. But it is quite possible to take each part separately and use what he has to say to gain an overview for a particular text. For example, the arguments of Gombrich and Goodman are by no means easy to follow, for various reasons, but Mitchell clarifies apparent contradictions and blindspots and, as a successful mediator should, enables his reader to go back to the original texts with renewed interest. Perhaps there will be others like myself who will be encouraged to tackle all the texts, because Mitchell's book also acts as a guide as well as being so intrinsically interesting.

And so to the books about picture-book form. One of the pioneering works is by Joseph H. Schwarcz, *Ways of the Illustrator, Visual Communication in Children's Literature*. He has a double approach to the illustrator's work as a means of symbolic communication. The two main concerns are: illustration as a work of visual art (that is, an aesthetic configuration with an expressive purpose) and the relation of illustration to the verbal text and how their joint representations reflect – explicitly and implicitly – aesthetic, psychological and educational attitudes.

Joseph H. Schwarcz
Ways of the Illustrator
American Library Association 1982

What Schwarcz does very successfully is to remind us of how many dimensions of the picture book there are to be considered. Not only does he give us an overview of the picture book and its role in our society, his book would be very useful for a student looking for an area for research: Schwarcz makes an order out of the chaos of possibilities. His authorial voice is clear, gently reminding us of our responsibilities towards children in our care.

More recently has come Perry Nodelman's *Words about Pictures: The Narrative Art of Children's Picture Books*. In his work, primarily semiotic in orientation, Nodelman discusses how the art and Art of the picture book form engage in the telling of stories, literal and metaphorical, and hypothesizes about how readers experience the picture book. Nodelman's work divides into two main areas: exclusively visual information and aspects of the relationships between words and pictures. His method is to draw upon an eclectic selection of strands from literary theory, psychology, and art philosophy, which, together with theories and process-models of his own, he applies to examples from well-known picture books.

Perry Nodelman
Words about Pictures
Univ. Georgia Press 1988

Broadly, Nodelman takes the view that the more knowledge a child has, the richer and more complex even very simple pictures become, and that children need to be taught how much more there is to pictures than an exclusive focus on the descriptive.

Following the material that is largely concerned with visual codes – easier to read than Arnheim – are three chapters which challenge our general understanding of what happens in reading a picture book with a text. These chapters represent Nodelman's pioneering achievement: a definition of the nature of the relationships between words and picture (which is different from Schwarcz's), a location for 'the essence of picture-book storytelling', and a process model for the rhythms of picture-book narrative.

Nodelman is a self-confessed words man, and I am not so happy with linguistic imperialism (Mitchell's phrase) as to accept that grasping the meaning of a picture is as neat a process as he suggests. However, his book is intended to teach the teacher, whom he leaves with the challenge of devising much-needed ways in which pedagogic practice may be deepened and widened. It was after reading Nodelman that I formalized my classroom practice and wrote the unit of work on picture books (pages 49-59).

Summary of Useful Terms

Art is not a science, and many of its terms have different applications and meanings, so the following list is meant only as a guide. Not every term listed below appears in the main text; all will be helpful in building up a working vocabulary for picture-book close looking.

abstract elements. What pictures are made from: lines, shapes, colours. The easiest way to think about abstract elements ('basic ingredients') is to restrict yourself to design on the flat surface of the paper. (If you have never done this before, it might help to turn the picture upside down, or reverse the image in a mirror: either will make you aware of the design for its own sake.) The design consists of interwoven arrangements of shapes, colour, lights and darks, a system of scale and intervals, an order of small- and large-scale relationships and rhythms. The design will be influenced by the artist's particular medium or mixed media, and (in the case of picture-book art) by the restraints of book publishing and methods of reproduction. We perceive the design or arrangement as an illusion of the world: as objects in space.

artist's style. A personal style is a particular way of using materials, of technique, of favouring certain pictorial effects. Style is always expressive and will reflect the artist's temperament (in how the marks are made), values (in the themes he chooses to explore) and relationship to a culture and historical period. The characteristics become evident through a body of work rather than a single picture book because an artist may adopt a historical style and display an influence in a particular work (like Sendak's nod to Winston Homer and Vergennes, Vermont, in *Mr Rabbit and the Lovely Present*). But if you look at that picture book alongside all the others by Sendak, the stylistic similarities are not at all difficult to find.

binding. The signatures (sections of pages of a book) are bound together by stitching or gluing. The binding results in a loss of picture area near the gutter (inner margins).

bleed. A picture 'bleeds' if it extends to the trimmed edge of the paper. A picture may bleed on one, two, three or all four edges. The effect suggests a life going on beyond the confines of the page so that the beholder becomes more of a participant in than a spectator of the pictured events.

bracelet shading. This is the line that follows the form to give the impression of volume. Forearms, legs, cloth curving around limbs or round the torso, tree trunks, and any cylindrical shape can be modelled by bracelet shading.

broken outline. Allows the ground space to enter the figure. The effect imparts a liveliness to the figure because the pen itself seems to have skipped over the paper as it made the marks. Works by Quentin Blake, Tony Ross and John Burningham furnish examples.

charcoal. Wood, often vine, is reduced by burning so that it can be used for drawing. The line produced by charcoal has a soft, powdery, sensuous quality.

collage. The technique of pasting cloth, paper, photographs, prints or other materials onto the picture surface (derived from the French verb *coller*, meaning 'to stick'). Collage is capable of generating visual tension since the materials draw attention to themselves for what they are, but at the same time the beholder is being asked to see them as part of the composition. A picture made entirely of collage has a static quality, and a master of the technique, like Ezra Jack Keats, will balance the flat two-dimensional pasted elements with areas of rich painting, as in *The Snowy Day*. Eric Carle often breaks the edge of his collaged shapes with drawn lines, crayon, paint, which gives the whole the suggestion of vitality.

colour. A colour has hue, tone and saturation.

hue denotes the different colours found on a scale ranging through red, orange, yellow, blue, green, indigo and violet, and is a way of distinguishing one colour from another. While an artist might refer to a hue as meaning the name of a pigment, for the rest of us 'hue' and 'colour' are interchangeable.

tone denotes the measure or degree of lightness or darkness of a coloured area, regardless of hue. We can separate tone from hue if we think of the area as being somewhere on a scale with absolute white at one extreme and absolute black at the other.

saturation is the term used to describe the degree of purity in a colour. A saturated red, for example, would be full, rich, intense. In painting, white is a saturated pigment. White is not used directly in printing because it is present as the colour of the paper. When we look at a picture-book illustration, a white area will appear very intense.

When mixed with black, a colour is said to be greyed or **muted** or called a **shade** – although in practice an artist who wanted subtle effects would not usually add black to shade a colour.

A colour mixed with white is called a **tint**. When an artist uses watercolour or transparent inks, the white paper has something of the same effect as mixing white with an opaque pigment.

Colour plays a role in the perception of space: it will advance or recede as it is changed by being made darker or lighter, warmer or cooler, more or less positive. The spatial relationships of forms, therefore, may be expressed through colour.

composite text. This is work that is made from the union of what the words say and what the pictures show. Properly speaking, it exists nowhere but in the reader/beholder's head.

continuous narrative. Shows one character portrayed in more than one place, and possibly in more than one setting, across a single picture plane. Satoshi Kitamura's *Ned and the Joybaloo* has many ingenious examples of this device.

contour. The external edge, or boundary or outline, of a form in drawing and painting. A contour line defines objects and gives them their precise structure and character.

crosshatching. Parallel strokes in one direction (hatching) are crossed with rows of parallel strokes at a different angle. Crosshatching is a means to achieve tone or different 'colours' of grey, with line, and has its origins in etching and engraving on metal, where it is used for shading and modelling. This traditional association with the past gives a certain gravitas, an old-fashioned air, to contemporary illustrations that are hatched and crosshatched. In addition, the technique literally has the effect of settling the image on the paper. Maurice Sendak's work is characterized by this use of line: see *Where the Wild Things Are*, *Higglety Pigglety Pop!*, *Hector Protector* and the incomparable drawings for *The Juniper Tree* to enjoy the technique in conjunction with colour and on its own.

doublespread. Except for the first and last pages, the story in a picture book is presented in a sequence of pairs of facing pages. The term **page opening** is used interchangeably to refer to the double-page unit of the picture-book form.

endpapers. The pages at either end of the book, one of which is glued to the inside of the front- and back-cover boards. Endpapers may be plain white or coloured, or printed with the artist's design. Kitamura provides extra opportunities for counting (sheep and stars) at either end of the hardback edition of *When Sheep Cannot Sleep*; Jane Hissey introduces her cast of characters in *Little Bear's Trousers*; a plain solid colour, like the chalky violet-grey chosen for Lisbeth Zwerger's *The Strange*

Child, prefigures the subtleties of both the artist's style and the story that is to follow.

figure. The shape or object portrayed as distinct from the (back)ground against which it is set. The terms **figure** and **ground** go together, and within one picture can be relative and changing. For example, in the illustration of Max in his bedroom (page 92), the moon can be seen as the figure against the background of the night sky, but also moon, sky and open window can be seen as the figure against the background of the blank wall.

form. A shape that is perceived as a three-dimensional object (whether person, animal or thing) may be referred to as a form. 'Form', 'figure' and 'image' may be used interchangeably in picture-book art. As the term implies, 'part form' describes an incomplete image.

format. Book size and book shape: **portrait** or **upright** is the term used for a book that is a vertical rectangle; **landscape** for a horizontal rectangle.

frame. A picture smaller than the page on which it appears is framed by the white margins of the paper (an **air frame**). Pictures may also be framed by decorative borders containing complementary images or by straight ruled or free-hand drawn lines of varying thickness and style. The quality of the frame affects the psychological meaning of what it surrounds. A rigid structure contains events while a free-hand drawn line appears less formal and allows for a livelier effect – as if the frame itself is breathing to the life of the pictured events. Contrast the two styles in Tony Ross's versions of *Jack the Giant Killer* and *Puss in Boots*. The rigid frames in the former do something to distance the truly brutal events depicted (and keep them safely penned in) while Puss pushes his luck, pushes events, and the fine-line frame flexes in response.

front matter. The title page (including title, name of author, illustrator, publisher), copyright page and any other printed material placed before the opening of a book's main text. Often called **prelims**.

gouache. An opaque water-based paint. Unlike watercolour it is possible to work from dark to light, adding white to lighten the colours. Water-thinned gouache can be used for graduated washes. So gouache allows an artist to reap one of the benefits of oil paint (putting in detailed highlights last) while retaining the spontaneity of watercolour. The threads of highlighting on Cloudy's fur and her whiskers show the effects of gouache (*Cloudy*, Deborah King).

84

ground. Plain, unfilled background area around figures.

gutter. The space of inner margin where two pages meet at the binding of a book. There is a slight loss of picture area near the gutter, where the pages are stitched or glued together, so a doublespread illustration presents a compositional challenge to the artist.

hatching. Parallel strokes in one direction, used to imply contour, depth or texture. When lines or strokes follow the form it is known as **bracelet shading**.

image. In the graphic sense means a likeness, a resemblance of the external form of an object. It can be used interchangeably with 'figure' and 'form' to refer to pictorial representations.

layout. Refers to the shape, size and arrangement of the illustrations and the placement of the text throughout the picture book. Layout plays a crucial role in the psychological effect upon the reader/beholder.

The most formal and traditional arrangement is an *entirely separate* presentation, with text and illustration on facing pages of the opening. The resulting visual rhythm, a series of strong beats, suits the folk- and fairy-tale form with its often repetitive structure, stereotypical characters, and its associations with settling down to hear a good story.

The text may be *partly integrated*, being superimposed upon the illustration in some instances and set apart above or below in others.

The arrangement which mirrors the inter-relationship of word and image is offered by the *wholly integrated layout*, where the segment of text is accommodated within the composition. In Deborah King's *Cloudy*, for example, the grey print is so close in tone to the picture in some places that, like the cat, it merges with the background, and the beholder is scarcely aware of its presence.

As to the shape, size and arrangement of the illustrations, the most static presentation is the plate; the most dynamic is a sequence showing the character in action over several closely presented frames, and possibly breaking an individual frame in what looks like a hurry to get out of it. Horizontal banding tends to suggest the passing of time or journeying. Look at Sendak's *In the Night Kitchen* to see how a supremely skilful layout seamlessly transports Mickey from bed to the kitchen, then over the Milky Way and into a milk bottle, down again, with a joyful refrain from the musical bakers and a climactic 'Cock a doodle doo!' from Mickey, bringing him back to bed with a satiated smile on his face.

line. Visible lines are used to create contour, tonal modelling, and a sign for movement. As well, lines have a character and life of their own: wiry, hesitant, nervous, bold, rapid, confident, sinuous, and so on.

Invisible lines of perceptual force affect the balance of pictures.

line effects.   In painting, line effects arise from changes of close colour. Look at the swirling skirts of the dancing gorillas in Anthony Browne's *Gorilla*. Line effects also appear in the record of brush strokes where they make patterns. See how the drag of the brush animates the surface of the picture of Cloudy streaking across the path of an oncoming car in *Cloudy*.

medium. The material the artist uses: pen, paints, crayons, pastels, and so on, which in themselves have colour and make shapes and lines. The term also applies to the picture itself (and, by extension, the picture book). In this usage the finished artwork is the medium for the artist's ideas and the channel between maker and beholder.

montage. A collection, an assembly of illustrations (or fragments of illustrations) arranged as a whole and, as a term, overlaps with collage. Raymond Briggs uses montage in *Gentleman Jim* to show simultaneously what is happening to his character (in small frames) as well as what he is thinking about (in large-scale superimposed vignettes), which results in the juxtaposition of Bronco lavatory rolls and a delectable supine Ingres odalisque.

overlapping. A simple depth cue, where foreground objects obscure the view of more distant objects.

page opening. See doublespread.

pastels. Dry colours. Powdered pigments are bound together with gum, made into sticks, and are used like crayons. Pastels are opaque, so mixing and modelling have to be done by crosshatching or juxtaposing dots of different colour. The effect is tactile, sensuous.

perspective. A graphic technique which creates the impression of depth and three dimensions on a two-dimensional surface.

linear perspective. The means of creating the sensation of depth or distance through the use of converging lines and vanishing points. For example, we are given the impression of a long hall or corridor through the lines which indicate the ceiling and floor area, walls and door placements in the illustration of Woolly in the empty house in *When Sheep Cannot Sleep*.

aerial perspective. Creates the sensation of depth by imitating modifications of colour which occur as a result of atmospheric effects. In *Outside Over There* Sendak suggests the far view across a river by lightening the tones and softening the detailing of the landscape beyond Mama's arbour wall.

pictorial means. What the artist makes the picture from: his materials and the effects which can be wrought from them.

pictorial style. A picture book will be presented in one of several broad categories of style: linear or graphic, painterly, line and colour in partnership, mixed media.

    linear or **graphic**. If what you are looking at is dominated by lines and linear rhythms, you have a descendant from the woodblock tradition. Charles Keeping is a classic example, whether he is working in black and white or with additional colour. Quentin Blake is another such artist. (The personal style of these artists is quite different because the marks each makes generate very different rhythms.) In a linear illustration modelling will come from contrasts and gradations of tone, by line (hatching and crosshatching).

    painterly. Illustrations that allow full play to more sensuous features such as contrasts and gradations of tone through colour and the possibilities offered by the medium itself, of overpainting, or scraping to reveal underpainting, of crackling or splattering the surface. Pastels, chalks, crayons as well as paint can make for painterly illustrations. Brian Wildsmith's work is essentially painterly.

    line and colour. In partnership: describes the style which is both linear (strongly defined and often closed outlines giving a hard edge to shapes) and painterly in its tonal modelling and textured surfaces and use of colour. Anthony Browne's pictorial style has these characteristics.

    mixed media. Applies to pictures made from the combined use of charcoal, ink, chalk, pastels, watercolour, gouache, wax, acrylics – two or more of any of these. Picture books in collage would come into this category.

picture plane. In a literal sense this refers to the flat surface of the picture. In a psychological sense it is also where the composition takes effect. The lines, shapes and colour have a dual role: on the surface and in depth. The ellipse on the surface is the circle in depth. The double function enables us to 'read' the ellipse as a table top in Max's bedroom in *Where the Wild Things Are*. We see what is there, and we 'see' by analogy on the picture plane.

plate. Although this term belongs to printing and photography, it is useful for describing a single illustration which, together with its frame (air or drawn), occupies all of one page. In effect it resembles both an enlarged photograph and the big pictures, or colour plates, which had to be 'tipped in' by hand in the gift books of the 1920s. Quarter, half and three-quarter plate describe framed illustrations of relatively smaller sizes.

recto. The right-hand page of a book.

running story. Refers to minor characters who appear throughout the sequence of pictures and who have a life of their own which flourishes independently alongside that of the main characters. The running story is never referred to in the text. In *Give a Dog a Bone* Brian Wildsmith introduces a quartet of tabbycats who inhabit the same town as the poor stray.

scale. The appearance, the illusion of size as opposed to the real or measured size. An organized use of scale depends upon the unity of certain proportions and the interval between shapes throughout the design.

shape. A two-dimensional outlined area in a picture that is regarded as an abstract element rather than what the shape represents. For example, 'Woolly's head and upper torso make a strong white triangular shape in contrast to the many horizontals in the composition' reveals that we are looking at structural relationships rather than objects.

signature. Large sheets of paper on which pages are printed, then folded and trimmed and bound into books. A group of pages made from one sheet is called a signature.

split narrative. Two episodes with different characters portrayed within the same setting on the picture plane. Anno teases Mr Fox with such a device more than once in *Anno's Aesop*, in illustrations for 'The Bear and the Traveller' and 'The Goat and the Donkey'.

texture. Though it is composed of lines, or blobs, and fills a form, texture is perceived as a general quality of surface and accordingly has strong associations with the sense of touch.

tonal modelling. Refers to the the artist's use of tone (light and shade) to model form (giving a shape the effect of solidity).

typography. The design of the whole book, including the choice of format, size, typeface, position of display lettering, length of lines (justified or unjustified), spacing between lines, break of lines to facilitate reading.

verso. Left-hand page of a book.

viewpoint. The position of the beholder in relation to the picture. The viewpoint establishes the point of view both literally and psychologically. A low viewpoint (worm's eye) gives an image an elevated importance as it appears to tower over the beholder. A high viewpoint (bird's eye) lays the world out at the beholder's feet. Multiple viewpoints at a fixed level send us travelling along the picture, while no fixed viewpoint has us wandering all over the surface. A good example of this last is Ida's journey in *Outside Over There*. Sendak gives his composition many centres of interest: sailors, Ida, the baby in a cave, goblins on rocks, a sleeping shepherd, Ida's mother in the arbour, a lamp, all of which may be seen to maximum advantage.

vignette. A small isolated design or illustration: it looks like a cut-out shape, traditionally in line, and more recently in line and colour as well. It is generally a decorative feature, and is often used to enliven a passage of text. The word comes from the French word for vine, and we can see examples of Arthur Rackham's clinging to the pages he illustrated for the *Fairy Tales of the Brothers Grimm*. See the dedication page of *In the Night Kitchen* with Mickey and his dough aeroplane for a vigorous modern example.

wash. A mixture of water with water-soluble paint, or coloured ink, which is applied in translucent layers on a ground of white paper. Its essential quality is transparency, with the white of the ground showing through the wash, even with the dark tones. Lisbeth Zwerger will show you how.

The printing process is outside the subject of this book. The easiest way to understand the way colour is reproduced by the printing press is to consult a children's book on the subject. *How a Book is Made* by Aliki, for instance, or David Macaulay's *The Way Things Work*, which shows the separation of the colours by the camera and the working of the offset press (and the subsequent binding process) with great clarity.

In order to illustrate further some of the terms in this summary, I have chosen two illustrations from the work of artists whose style makes a contrast with that of Satoshi Kitamura and Deborah King. The black and white reproductions enable me to pinpoint certain areas, but the commentary refers to the full-colour pictures in *Gorilla* and *Where the Wild Things Are*.

Gorilla
© 1983 Anthony Browne

I call this illustration a **plate**. The colour scheme is in **hues** of red, yellow and blue – primary colours, which have a high level of **saturation** (intensity, strength of colour) and which promote a cheerful effect. Hannah's left pyjama leg is the most saturated colour.

Looking at the illustration in this black and white reproduction

90

gives us a general idea of the tonal scheme of the composition, although the finer distinctions are lost. The camera distorts tone values when photographing strong colours. For example, the different tones of Hannah's red clothing and her father's are not as apparent in the picture-book illustration as in this black and white reproduction. It is very difficult to judge the tonal quality of strong colours: painters are always squinting because it helps them to judge. Looking at the full-colour illustration, however, we can easily see that light and medium **tones** predominate.

The colour of the wallpaper is a yellow **tint**. Whether Anthony Browne mixed white pigment with the yellow or whether the effect of a tint is the result of the transparency of the paint on the white paper beneath, I cannot tell.

Bracelet shading gives the impression of volume: a soft material gathering in the folds over the curve of Hannah's arm. The **line effect** is created by colour, possibly a crayon in conjunction with the paint. The creases on top of the father's jeans act as a very clear example of the effect: block out the creases with your fingers and the legs become two flat planes.

Our **viewpoint** is difficult to judge because there are no converging lines to make use of. Browne seems deliberately to create a hieratic quality with his side views and very little indication of depth (no **linear perspective** and the very minimum of **overlapping**). There is visual tension between the carefully observed, detailed **figures** against a simplified and flattened **ground**: the figures appear still and frozen in time. Their arrangement, side by side, echoes the child's drawing on the wall.

Making the most of what clues we have, our viewpoint is a little to the right of centre of the picture and level with the top of the table. If the viewpoint were higher, we could see something of the table top, and if lower, we couldn't see the seat of the chair. Browne has depicted Hannah and her father on a relatively large **scale**, which closes the distance between picture and beholder. We see the two characters, the table and chair and the skirting board as **part forms**.

Browne has used a closed outline for all the forms, although the contour becomes less distinct at the top of the father's head and at the edge of Hannah's pony-tail.

Max's form faces left and, from the direction, is understood as coming back from his adventures; his form faces right when he sets out.

We see the colour as a transparent tint or wash under a drawing – not as coloured shapes as in the Anthony Browne picture. Sendak has used greyed or **muted** colours, which have low saturation and which appear pale and dim or dark and dull. This effect sustains the dreamlike quality of the experience being portrayed. The **tones** are lightest on the bed cover, top of the pillows, and the front of Max's figure, and on the moon with its reflected light striking the window frame and table top.

The quality of Sendak's **line** defies easy description. There are many variations in the **contour** alone. It is so broken and light in

92

weight on the falls of the bed linen that edges are fluid – lost and found. Myriads of marks of thread-like fineness in the corner of the room where the shadows are deep result in the contour of the tablecloth being held by hints of colour rather than an **outline**. The contour on Max's form is simple, firm, restrained; as if the edge had been felt for, then set down. There seems to have been no haste in making the marks, but rather a controlled pleasure. I have no doubt that to see the original drawings would be an absorbing and rewarding experience.

Examples follow of how Sendak creates different effects from lines.

Large areas are **crosshatched**, which has the effect of lowering the tone of the colour beneath it and settling the image on the paper. The crosshatching on the walls is drawn in perspective and creates the illusion of depth, so it is doing two things at once.

Line for texture – a surface quality

Hatching in long broken lines represents the grain of the wooden bedstead.

Very fine curvular lines give Max's tail a short-hair, curly, fluffy texture, with longer soft hair at the tip.

Very short, very dense lines suggest a cropped head of hair.

Faint long broken lines on areas which are turned from the light and the closed outline suggest that Max's body-suit is made from a soft cloth.

The curving clumps of short lines on the carpet give the impression of a long-tufted carpet, and the swirling painted lines increase the suggestion of depth without making the tone of the colour much darker.

Lines to create tone

Sendak uses lines to graduate tone.

The fine curving lines on the pillow shape cause it to appear plump.

Shadows where the form of an object turns away from the light source are created by crosshatching, which is curved like bracelet shading so that the lines indicate roundness on door knob, bedposts, flower pot.

Line as a sign for movement

The variation in density and the direction of the lines imply movement in the tail as a whole.

The change in length and direction of the lines of Max's left arm and what we can see of the palm of his left hand make

93

between them a sign for the flex of Max's wrist.

Line and perspective

Very strange things happen with the perspective, whether intentionally or instinctively on Sendak's part. The door, given the way he has drawn it, would be at least six feet wide. The carèfully contrived three-dimensional effect of walls, floor and ceiling in linear perspective throw into contrast irregularities of perspective in the view of the bed: its structure is out of alignment and the long bed leg on the far right of the picture twists and distorts the space and increases the feeling that 'things aren't quite what they seem to be', which accords with the notion of a bedpost which reverts to a tree.

Also there is a conflict between moonlight and roomlight: the cast shadows of bed, table and figure are ambiguous. For the moonlight to hit the sides of the window frames as it does, the moon as well as the moonlight has come into the room.

Despite the cumulative effect of playing so freely, graphically, with what we know of 'reality', the composition's **linear emphases**, which are vertical and horizontal, give stability to the whole.

Indexed Booklist

The picture books mentioned and discussed are arranged alphabetically by artist. The year date refers to the first publication in Britain. Where illustrations have been reproduced from books originated in other countries, their original publishers are also indicated.